SIMÓN BOLÍVAR, THE LIBERATOR

SIMÓN BOLÍVAR, THE LIBERATOR

PATRIOT, WARRIOR, STATESMAN
FATHER OF FIVE NATIONS

A SKETCH OF HIS LIFE AND HIS WORK

GUILLERMO A. SHERWELL

A SHERWELL BOOK

Published by Wildside Press LLC.
www.wildsidebooks.com

NOTE

Guillermo A. Sherwell (1878-1926) was the recipient of Doctorate Degrees from the National University of Mexico and from the University of Georgetown. Among the posts which he filled was that of Rector of the National University of Mexico, Legal Counsellor of the Inter-American Committee in Washington and Professor of History and of Hispano-American literature. Sincerely interested in the heroes of Spanish-American independence, he dedicated himself to the study of their lives and especially to that of the Liberator. He also wrote a biography of Sucre.

This biography of Bolívar was first published in Washington in 1921. It was again published in Baltimore in 1930. There have been two translations into Spanish, that of Roberto Cortázar and that of R. Cansinos-Assens, published respectively in Bogotá (1922 and 1930) and in Madrid (1922).

The Bolivarian Society of Venezuela has decided that in homage to the memory of the Liberator on the occasion of the transfer of the statue in New York to its new site at the head of the Avenue of the Americas, the publication of another edition of this excellent work of Mr. Sherwell's which gives in an excellent condensed form the historical significations of Bolívar. The children of Mr. Sherwell have kindly given their consent to the publication of this edition which is made under the auspices of the Junta de Gobierno of the United States of Venezuela.

INTRODUCTION

In the history of peoples, the veneration of national heroes has been one of the most powerful forces behind great deeds. National consciousness, rather than a matter of frontiers, racial strain or community of customs, is a feeling of attachment to one of those men who symbolize best the higher thoughts and aspirations of the country and most deeply impress the hearts of their fellow citizens. Despite efforts to write the history of peoples exclusively from the social point of view, history has been, and will continue to be, mainly a record of great names and great deeds of national heroes.

The Greeks, for us and for themselves, are not so much the people who lived in the various city-states of Hellas, nor the people dominated and more or less influenced by the Romans and later the Mohammedan conquerors, nor even the present population in which the old pure Hellenic element is in a proportion much smaller than is generally thought. Greece is what she is, lives in the life of men and shapes the minds and souls of peoples, through her great heroes, through her various gods, which were nothing but divinized heroes. Greece is for us Apollo, as a symbol of whatever is filled with light, high, beautiful and noble; Heracles for what is strength, energy, organization, life as it should be lived by human beings. Leonidas stands for us as a symbol of heroic deeds; Demosthenes as a symbol of the convincing powers of oratory and Pericles as the crystallization of Grecian life in its totality of beauty, learning and social and civic life. Greece is a type, is an attitude, is a protest against oppression, is an aspiration towards beauty, is an inspiration and a guide for men who live in the higher planes of feeling and thought. But Greece is not all that as a people; Greece is all that through men converted into symbols.

So it is with other peoples.

Rome still signifies for us the defense of the bridge against the powerful enemy; a man taking absolute power over the State and then surrendering it to the people from whom it came. Rome is Repúblican virtue, and imperial power,—and also, alas! imperial degradation. Imperial Rome represents persecution of religion which does not recognize Caesar as a god and the assimilation of religions which do not hesitate to add a god to those they adore. Rome, too, symbolizes the tendency to unity which survives and inspires the life of the nations of Europe, if not of the world,—a tendency altogether manifest in the last gigantic struggle through which mankind has just passed. Rome, finally, stands for Law, for the most marvelous social machine ever devised by human brains. But Rome is all that, and more than that, through Horace, Sulla, Cato, Caesar, Cicero, Nero, Caracalla and Justinian.

The confusion of the Middle Ages has some points of light, always around a man. The great Frederic Barbarossa stands for Germany, as does William Tell for Switzerland, as Ivan the Great for Russia, as the Cid for Spain, as King Arthur for England and Charlemagne for France.

The modern peoples, those who only lately have begun to live as nations, have their heroes, who perhaps do not seem so great to us as the old heroes, because they have not been magnified by time; but, if compared with men of the past, many of them are as great, if not, in some cases, greater. The countries of America are at present forming this tradition about their illustrious ancestors. And, if they want to live the strong life of the nations destined to last and to be powerful and respected, they must persevere in the work of building up around their fathers the frame-work of their national consciousness. Washington every day appears nobler to us, because every day we understand better what is the meaning of his sacrifice and his work; every day we learn to appreciate more the value of the inheritance he left to us when he gave us a free country where we can think and speak and work, untrammeled by the whims and caprices of foreign masters. And the nations to the south of us are also building their national consciousness around their great heroes, among them the greatest of all, Bolívar, one of those men who appear in the world at long intervals, selected by God to be the leaders of multitudes, to be performers of miracles, achieving what is impossible for the common man. They live a life of constant inspiration, as if they were not guided by their own frail judgment, but, like Moses, by the smoke and the flame of God through a desert, through suffering and success, through happiness and misfortune, until they might see before them the Promised Land of Victory, some destined to enjoy the full possession of it, and others to die with no other happiness than that of leaving an inheritance to their successors.

These few pages, devoted to the life and work of Simón Bolívar, the great South American Liberator, will attain their object if the reader understands and appreciates how unusual a man Bolívar was. Every citizen of the United States of America must respect and venerate his sacred memory, as the Liberator and Father of five countries, the man who assured the independence of the rest of the South American peoples of Spanish speech; the man who conceived the plans of Pan-American unity which those who came after him have elaborated, and the man who, having conquered all his enemies and seen at his feet peoples and laws, effected the greatest conquest, that of himself, sacrificing all his aspirations and resigning his power, to go and die, rewarded by the ingratitude of those who owed him their existence as free men. The more the life of this man is studied, the greater he appears, and the nearer he seems to the superhuman.

The American people, made free by Washington, do not begrudge the legitimate glory of other illustrious men, and if they have not rendered up to this time the homage due to Simón Bolívar, it has been mainly through lack of accurate knowledge of his wonderful work. The city of New York, the greatest community in the world, is now honoring his memory by placing in a conspicuous section of its most beautiful park a statue which the Government of Venezuela has given it; the statue of the Man of the South, the brother in glory to our own Washington. No greater homage could be paid to him than to have American fathers and mothers pass by the noble monument, pointing out to their children the statue and telling them the marvelous story of Simón Bolívar.

In a book as brief as this it is impossible to present documents or to give long quotations. Nevertheless, we may fairly affirm that all statements herein made are substantiable by documentary evidence. We have consulted all the books and pamphlets which have been at hand and have studied both sides of debatable questions regarding Bolívar. To follow a chronological order we have been guided by the beautiful biography written by Larrazábal, the man called by F. Lorain Petre "the greatest flatterer of Bolívar." That this assertion is false is proved in the first volume cited below. Petre's monograph contains apparent earmarks of impartiality, but in reality it is nothing but a bitter attack on the reputation of Bolívar. Its translator, a distinguished Venezuelan writer, is to be thanked for the serenity with which he has destroyed his imputations. We find nothing to add in defense of the Liberator.

The following studies have been particularly consulted:

"Bolívar por los más grandes escritores americanos, precedido de un estudio por Miguel de Unamuno," Madrid and Buenos Aires, 1914, a book containing the following monographs:

"Simón Bolívar," by Juan Montalvo (Ecuadorian)
"Simón Bolívar," by F. García Calderón (Peruvian)
"Simón Bolívar," by P.M. Arcaya (Venezuelan)
"Bolívar y su campaña de 1821," by General L. Duarte Level (Mexican)[1]
"Bolívar en el Perú," by A. Galindo (Colombian)
"Simón Bolívar," by B. Vicuña Mackenna (Chilean)
"Simón Bolívar," by J.B. Alberdi (Argentinean)
"Simón Bolívar," by José Martí (Cuban)

1 Duarte Level is not Mexican but Venezuelan.

"El ideal internacional de Bolívar," by Francisco José Urrutia (Colombian)

"La entrevista de Guayaquil," by Ernesto de la Cruz (Chilean)

"Bolívar, escritor," by Blanco-Fombona (Venezuelan)

"Bolívar," by F. Lorain Petre (North American)[2]

"Bolívar," by J.E. Rodó (Uruguayan)

"Bolívar, íntimo," by Cornelio Hispano (Colombian)

"Bolívar, profesor de energía," by José Veríssimo (Brazilian)

"Bolívar, legislador," by Jorge Ricardo Vejarano (Colombian)

"Discursos y Proclamas—Simón Bolívar," R. Blanco-Fombona, Paris.

"Documentos para la Vida Pública del Libertador" por Blanco y Azpurúa, Caracas.

"El Libertador de la América del Sur," Guzmán Blanco, London, 1885.

"Estudio Histórico," Aristides Rojas, Caracas, 1884.

"La Creación de un Continente," F. García Calderón, Paris.

"La Entrevista de Bolívar y San Martín en Guayaquil," Camilo Destruge, Guayaquil, 1918.

"La última enfermedad, los últimos momentos y los funerales de Simón Bolívar," Dr. A.P. Révérend, Paris, 1866.

"Leyendas Históricas," A. Rojas, Caracas, 1890.

"Memorias de O'Leary," translated from English by Simón B. O'Leary, Caracas, 1883.

"Orígenes del Gran Mariscal de Ayacucho," discursos del Señor D. Felipe Francia, Caracas, 1920.

"Papeles de Bolívar," Vicente Lecuna, Caracas, 1917.

"Pensamientos consagrados a la memoria del Libertador," Caracas, 1842.

"Recuerdos del Tiempo Heróico—Pájinas de la vida militar i política del Gran Mariscal de Ayacucho," José María Rey de Castro, Guayaquil, 1883.

"Resúmen de la Historia de Venezuela," Baralt y Díaz, Paris, 1841.

"Simón Bolívar," Arturo Juega Farrulla, Montevideo, 1915.

"Vida de Simón Bolívar," Larrazábal, Madrid, 1918; also sixth edition of same book, New York, Andres Cassard, 1883.

For the use of various documents, articles, and papers, we are also indebted to Dr. Manuel Segundo Sánchez, Director of the National Library of Caracas, Venezuela, as well as to Dr. Julius Goebel of the University of Virginia for his kindness in letting us examine his notes on certain papers existing in the files of the State Department in Washington.

We beg to express our sincere gratitude to Miss Edith H. Murphy of Bay Ridge High School and St. Joseph College of Brooklyn, and to Dr. C.E. McGuire of the Inter American High Commission, for their revision

2 Lorain Petre is not North American but English.

of the original manuscript and their very valuable suggestions regarding the subject matter and the style.

For the appreciations and judgments appearing in this monograph, its author assumes full responsibility.

CHAPTER I

THE SPANISH COLONIES IN AMERICA

Everybody knows that America was discovered by Christopher Columbus, who served under the King and Queen of Spain, and who made four trips, in which he discovered most of the islands now known as the West Indies and part of the central and southern regions of the American continent. Long before the English speaking colonies which now constitute the United States of America were established, the Spaniards were living from Florida and the Mississippi River to the South, with the exception of what is now Brazil, and had there established their culture, their institutions and their political system.

In some sections, the Indian tribes were almost exterminated, but generally the Spaniards mingled with the Indians, and this intercourse resulted in the formation of a new race, the mixed race (mestizos) which now comprises the greater number of the inhabitants of what we call Latin America.

African slavery added another racial element, which is often discernible in the existing population.

The Latin American peoples today are composed of European whites, American whites (Creoles), mixed races of Indian and white, white and Negro, Negro and Indian, Negro and mestizo, and finally, the pure Indian race, distinctive types of which still appear over the whole continent from Mexico to Chile, but which has disappeared almost entirely in Uruguay and Argentina. Some countries have the Indian element in larger proportions than others, but this distribution of races prevails substantially all over the continent.

It would distract us from our purpose to give a full description of the grievances of the Spanish colonies in America. They were justified and it is useless to try to defend Spain. Granting that Spain carried out a wonderful work of civilization in the American continent, and that she is entitled to the gratitude of the world for her splendid program of colonization, it is only necessary, nevertheless, to cite some of her mistakes of administration in order to prove the contention of the colonists that they must be free.

Books could not be published or sold in America without the permission of the Consejo de Indias, and several cases were recorded of severe punishment of men who disobeyed this rule. Natives could not avail themselves of the advantages of the printing press. Communication and trade with foreign nations were forbidden. All ships found in American waters without license from Spain were considered enemies. Nobody, not even the Spaniards, could come to America without the permission of the King, under penalty of loss of property and even of loss of life. Spaniards, only, could trade, keep stores or sell goods in the streets. The Indians and mestizos could engage only in mechanical trades.

Commerce was in the hands of Spain, and taxes were very often prohibitive. Even domestic commerce, except under license, was forbidden. It was especially so regarding the commerce between Perú and New Spain, and also with other colonies. Some regulations forbade Chile and Perú to send their wines and other products to the colonists of the North. The planting of vineyards and olive trees was forbidden. The establishment of industry, the opening of roads and improvements of any kind were very often stopped by the Government. Charles IV remarked that he did not consider learning advisable for America.

Americans were often denied the right of public office. Great personal service or merit was not sufficient to destroy the dishonor and disgrace of being an American.

The Spanish colonies were divided into vice-royalties and general captaincies. There were also *audiencias*, which existed under the vice-royalties and general captaincies. The Indians were put under the care and protection of Spanish officials called *encomenderos*, but these in fact, in most cases, were merciless exploiters of the natives who, furthermore, were subject to many local disabilities. The Kings of Spain tried to protect the Indians, and many laws were issued tending to spare them from the ill-treatment of the Spanish colonists. But the distance from Spain to America was great, and when laws and orders reached the colonies, they never had the force which they were intended to have when issued. There existed a general race hatred. The Indians and the mestizos, as a rule, hated the Creoles, or American whites, who often were as bad as, or even worse than, the Spanish colonists in dealing with the aborigines. It is not strange, then, that in a conflict between Spain and the colonies, the natives should take sides against the Creoles, who did most of the thinking, and who were interested and concerned with all the changes through which the Spanish nation might pass, and that they would help Spain against the white promoters of the independent movement. This assertion must be borne in mind to understand the difficulties met by the independent leaders, who had to fight not only against the Spanish army, which was in reality never very large, but also against the natives of their own land. To regard this as an invariable condition would nevertheless lead to error, for at times, under proper guidance, the natives would pass to the files of the insurgent leaders and fight against the Spaniards.

Furthermore, it is necessary to remember that education was very limited in the Spanish colonies; that in some of them printing had not been introduced, and that its introduction was discouraged by the public authority; and that public opinion, which even at this time is so poorly developed, was very frequently poorly informed in colonial times, or did not exist, unless we call public opinion a mass of prejudices, superstitions and erroneous habits of thinking fostered by interests, either personal or of the government.

This was the condition of the Spanish American countries at the beginning of the nineteenth century, full of agitation and conflicting ideas, when new plans of life for the people were being elaborated and put into practice as experiments on which many men founded great hopes and which many others feared as forerunners of a general social disintegration.

CHAPTER II

1783-1810: BOLÍVAR'S EARLY LIFE. VENEZUELA'S FIRST ATTEMPT TO OBTAIN SELF-GOVERNMENT.

Simón Bolívar was born in the city of Caracas on the twenty-fourth day of July, 1783; his father was don Juan Vicente Bolívar, and his mother, doña María de la Concepción Palacios y Blanco. His father died when Simón was still very young, and his mother took excellent care of his education. His teacher, afterwards his intimate friend, was don Simón Rodríguez, a man of strange ideas and habits, but constant in his affection and devotion to his illustrious pupil.

Bolívar's family belonged to the Spanish nobility, and in Venezuela was counted in the group called Mantuano, or noble. They owned great tracts of land and lived in comfort, associating with the best people, among whom they were considered leaders.

The early youth of Bolívar was more or less like that of the other boys of his city and station, except that he gave evidence of a certain precocity and nervousness of action and speech which distinguished him as an enthusiastic and somewhat idealistic boy.

Misfortune taught Bolívar its bitter lessons when he was still young. At fifteen years of age he lost his mother. Then his uncle and guardian, don Carlos Palacios, sent him to Madrid to complete his education. The boat on which he made the trip left La Guaira on January 17, 1799, and stopped at Vera Cruz. This enabled young Simón Bolívar to go to Mexico City and other towns of New Spain. In the capital of the colony he was treated in a manner becoming his social standing, and met the highest officials of the government. The viceroy had several conversations with him, and admired his wit; but it finally alarmed him when the boy came to talk on political questions and, with an assurance superior to his age, defended the freedom of the American colonies.

Bolívar lived in Madrid with his relatives, and had occasion to be in touch with the highest members of the court, and even with the King, Charles IV, and the Queen. There he met a young lady named María Teresa Toro, whose uncle, the Marquis of Toro, lived in Caracas and was a friend of the young man. He fell in love with her, but as he was only seventeen years old, the Marquis of Ustáriz, who was in charge of Bolívar in Madrid, advised him to delay his plans for an early marriage.

In 1801 Bolívar went to Paris, where he found Napoleon Bonaparte, as First Consul, undertaking his greatest labors of social reorganization after the long period of anarchy through which France had passed following the Revolution. Bonaparte was one of the most admired men at that time. He had come back from Egypt and Syria, had been victorious at Marengo and Hohenlinden, and had just signed the Peace of Lunéville. One does not wonder that Bolívar should admire him and that his letters should contain many expressions of enthusiasm about the great man of Europe.

In the same year he returned to Madrid and married María Teresa Toro, deciding to go back at once to Venezuela with his wife, to live peacefully, attending to his own personal business and property. But again fate dealt him a hard blow and shattered all the dreams and plans of the young man. His virtuous wife died in January, 1803, ten months after their arrival in Caracas. He had not yet reached his twenty-first year, and had already lost father, mother and wife. His nerves became steeled and his heart prepared for great works, for works requiring the concentration of mind which can be given only by men who have no intimate human connections or obligations. As a South American orator lately declared:[3] "Neither Washington nor Bolívar was destined to have children of his own, so that we Americans might call ourselves their children."

Bolívar decided immediately to leave for Europe. Nothing could keep him in his own country. He had loved his wife and his wife only could have led him to accept a life of ease and comfort. He decided never to marry again and, perhaps to assuage the pain in his heart, he decided to devote his time to the study of the great problems of his country, and to bend all his energies and strength to their solution. At the end of 1803, he was again in Madrid, giving his wife's father the sad news of their great loss.

From Madrid, Bolívar went to Paris, and was in the city when the Empire was established. All the admiration the man of the Republic had won from Bolívar immediately crumbled to dust before the young American. "Since Napoleon has become a king," said Bolívar, "his glory to me seems like the brilliancy of hell." He did not attend the ceremony of Napoleon's coronation, and made him the object of bitter attacks when among his own friends. He never hesitated to speak of the liberty of America with all his acquaintances, who enjoyed his conversation in spite of the ideas that he supported.

In the spring of 1805 he went on a walking tour to Italy, with his teacher and friend, don Simón Rodríguez. In Milan he saw Napoleon crowned as King of Italy, and then witnessed a great parade passing

3 Atilano Carnevali, on the occasion of placing a wreath before Washington's statue in Caracas, July 4, 1920.

before the French Emperor. All these royal ceremonies increased his hatred of monarchy.

From Milan he went to Florence, Venice, Rome and Naples, studying everything, informing himself of all the currents of public opinion, and dreaming of what he intended to accomplish for his own people. While in Rome, he and his teacher went to Mount Aventin. There they denounced in an intimate talk the oppression of peoples and discussed the liberty of their native Venezuela. When their enthusiasm had reached its highest pitch, the young dreamer took the hand of his master, and at that historic spot, he made a solemn vow to free his country.

From Italy, he came to the United States, where he visited Boston, New York, Philadelphia and other towns, sailing from Charleston for Venezuela. He arrived in Caracas at the end of 1806.

Upon his return home, Bolívar devoted himself to the care and improvement of his estate. Yet his ideas continued to seethe, especially when the constant spectacle of the state of affairs in Venezuela stimulated this ferment of his mind.

Among the American colonies, Venezuela was not considered by Spain as one of the most important. Mexico and Perú, celebrated by their production of mineral wealth, were those which attracted most of the attention of the Spaniards. Venezuela was apparently poor, and certainly did not contribute many remittances of gold and silver to the mother country. It had been organized as a captaincy general in 1731, after having been governed in different ways and having had very little communication with Spain. It is said that from 1706 to 1722, not a single boat sailed from any Venezuelan port for Spain. Commercial intercourse between the provinces was forbidden, and local industries could not prosper because the purchase of the products of Spanish industries was compulsory for the natives, at prices set after all transportation expenses and high taxes were taken into account. The colonists were oppressed by taxes and kept in ignorance.

This state of affairs had produced a latent feeling of irritation and a desire for a change. The native white population read the books of the French philosophers, especially those of Rousseau and Montesquieu. The ideas proclaimed by the United States of America and those preached by the most radical men of the French Revolution were smuggled in and known in spite of prohibition.

At the middle of the eighteenth century, there had been a movement against the Compañía Guipuzcoana, established about 1730, and which greatly oppressed the people. This movement failed and its leaders were severely punished.

At the end of the eighteenth century, Spain allied herself with England to fight against France. This war ended in 1795 with the Treaty of Basel, by which Spain lost Santo Domingo to France. A year later, Spain allied herself with France against England, and the disastrous war which followed resulted in the loss of the island of Trinidad to England, by the Treaty of Amiens, in 1802. France and England used these possessions to foster revolutions in the Spanish colonies.

In 1797 a conspiracy was started in Caracas, but it too failed. Some of its leaders received death sentences, others were expelled from the country and others were imprisoned. In Mexico, in Perú and in the southernmost part of the continent, men were working in favor of the idea of freedom.

In Europe, at this time, there was a very prominent Venezuelan, don Francisco Miranda, who had played an important rôle in the world events of that period. Miranda was born in Caracas, came to the North American colonies, and fought under Washington against the English power. Afterwards he went to Europe and fought in the armies of revolutionary France, attaining the rank of general. His friends were among the most distinguished men in Europe in political position or international achievement. He talked to them tirelessly, trying to convert them to the idea of the necessity for emancipating the countries of America. He failed to receive the attention he desired in England, and came to America. In New York he prepared an expedition and went to Venezuela, arriving there in March of 1806, with three boats, some arms, ammunition and men. He found the Spaniards prepared, and was defeated, losing two of his ships and many men as prisoners. He escaped with the other boat to Trinidad. In the West Indies he obtained the help of an English admiral, Sir A. Cochrane, and with larger forces returned to Venezuela, landing at Coro, which he took in August, 1806. But there he found the greatest enemy with which he and Bolívar had to contend, and that was the lack of the sanction of public opinion. Men whom Miranda had expected to increase his army failed to appear, and perhaps this indifference was aggravated by the antipathy with which the natives saw the foreign element which predominated in Miranda's army. Lacking the support of the people and the reserves which Miranda had expected to get from the English colony of Jamaica, he withdrew and went to London, altogether discouraged.

At that time great changes had occurred in Spain. Charles IV, its weak monarch, saw the French army invading his country under the pretense of going to Portugal, and feared that Napoleon would end by wresting the Spanish throne from him. If he allied himself with Napoleon, England could easily seize America, and should he ally himself with England, he would make an enemy of Napoleon, who already was in possession of Spain itself. The Crown Prince of Spain, Fernando, was intriguing against his father, and Charles IV had him imprisoned. Then it was discovered that the Prince was in treacherous relations with the ministers of Napoleon. The King complained to the French Emperor, who persuaded him to forgive and release his son. Meanwhile, the French army was advancing into Spain while the English were fomenting among the Spanish people the hatred for the French. The latter availed themselves of their advantageous position and, feeling sure of their strength in Spanish lands, demanded from the Court the cession of the northern section of Spain contiguous to Portugal. Rumors ran wild in the Court, and it was even said that the monarch and his family would leave Spain for Mexico. A favorite of the King, named Manuel Godoy, received the greatest blame for this situation, and Fernando, the Crown Prince, being the main antagonist of Godoy, was regarded as the champion of Spanish right and was loved by the Spanish people. The people rose and demanded that Godoy should be delivered to them. In March, 1808, the King abdicated and Fernando was proclaimed King. But the abdication was insincere, and Charles IV wrote to Napoleon that he had been compelled to take that action, certain that if he did not do so, he and the Queen would perish. Not content with this communication, Charles IV went to Bayonne to meet Napoleon, where his son Fernando had been invited by Napoleon to meet him. There one of the most disgraceful episodes in Spanish history occurred. Fernando renounced his rights to his father, and then his father renounced his rights and those of his family to Napoleon and to whomever he might select to rule. Napoleon immediately made his brother Joseph King of Spain. This occurred in May, 1808. The Spanish people had never been taken into consideration in all these dealings. But they wanted to be considered and they decided that they would be. Murat was governor in Madrid, and on May 2 the people rebelled against him. Great carnage ensued. Though the rebellion was suppressed, the fire burning in the Spanish soul was not extinguished. Everywhere *juntas provinciales* (provincial assemblies) were organized against the intruder; they allied themselves with England and declared that Fernando VII was the legitimate King of Spain and that the nation was at war with France. In order to unify the actions of the different juntas, a central junta was established in Aranjuez on September 25, 1808.

All these events had a tremendous effect in the American colonies. News was received in Venezuela of the abdication of Charles and Fernando, with orders to the colonies to recognize the new government. But at the same time an English boat sent by Admiral Cochrane arrived, and announced to the Venezuelan authorities the establishment of the juntas and the organization of resistance to the French. The authorities concluded to obey the orders brought by the French messengers, but the people rose in Caracas as in Spain, went to the city council and forced it to proclaim Fernando VII the legitimate monarch of Spain, thus starting a revolution, which in its inception had all the appearance of loyalty to the reigning house of Spain, but which very soon was transformed into a real movement of emancipation.

Some days later the city council asked the governor to establish a junta in Caracas, similar to those already established in Spain. The Spanish authorities wanted to have recognized the supremacy of the junta assembled in Seville, Spain, which had assumed the name of Supreme Junta of Spain and her Colonies. The Venezuelans insisted that they should have a junta in Caracas, and in order to foster this idea the most prominent leaders of public thought met secretly at the house of Simón Bolívar. Most of the conspirators were young men, united by strong ties of friendship or family. Among them were the Marquis of Toro and don José Félix Ribas, a relative of Bolívar, two very distinguished men. The meetings were sometimes held at the house of Ribas. It was not long before they were discovered. They determined to petition for the establishment of a junta in Caracas. The authorities ordered them to be put into prison; and in spite of their efforts, the Supreme Junta of Spain and her Colonies was recognized in January, 1809. The Junta Central declared in that same month that all the Spanish colonies formed part of the Spanish monarchy itself, which statement apparently was a declaration of equality. However, in fact, it was not so, since the elections of deputies to the junta were not to be made by the people but by the captain general, advised by the city council. The representation was also very disproportionate. The deputies for Spain were to number 36 while those for America only 12.

In May of that year, a new captain general, don Vicente Emparan, arrived in Venezuela. This man was more imperious than his predecessors had been, and immediately alienated the good will of the city council and the audiencia. He set up still greater obstacles to commerce, sent many prominent men into exile, declared criminals those who received printed matter from abroad, and established an organized system of espionage.

In 1810, when Emparan was exercising his power with the strongest hand, the patriots were meeting in the country wherever they could under different pretexts, in order to organize themselves and to work for their ideals. Bolívar was on the point of being exiled; many prominent men were either imprisoned or sent out of Caracas. The French armies seemed to conquer all opposition in Spain, and the Junta Central had been forced to take refuge in Cádiz. Rumors were circulated that Cádiz had fallen into the hands of the French. Then the patriots decided to wait no longer, and Bolívar, Ribas and other friends planned to take immediate steps.

On the morning of April 19, 1810, Holy Thursday, the city council assembled to attend the religious services in the cathedral, and Emparan was invited to be present. Before leaving for the service, the council told the governor that it was necessary to establish in Venezuela a government of its own in order to defend the country and the rights of the legitimate monarch. The governor answered that he would consider the matter after the service, and left the council. On arriving at the church he was stopped by a patriot called Francisco Salias who asked him to return to the council, declaring that the public welfare so required. Emparan saw that the troops were not ready to support him and, willingly or not, went back to the hall, where he yielded to everything that was proposed to him. Emparan was deposed and the first locally chosen government of Spanish America was established. The principle that the provinces of America possessed the right of self-government, since no general government existed, was proclaimed.

CHAPTER III

1811-1812: THE DECLARATION OF INDEPENDENCE, JULY 5, 1811. MIRANDA'S FAILURE.

The first acts of the Junta were acts of moderation and wisdom. Emparan and other Spanish authorities were expelled from the country. The Spaniards were assured that they would be treated as brothers, with the same consideration as all Americans. The Junta sent notice of this movement to the other countries of the continent in the following lofty words:

> "Venezuela has placed herself in the number of free nations, and hastens to give advice of this event to her neighbors so that, if the aspirations of the new world are in accord with hers, they might give her help in the great and very difficult career she has undertaken. 'Virtue and moderation' have been our motto. 'Fraternity, union and generosity' should be yours, so that these great principles combined may accomplish the great work of raising America to the political dignity which so rightly belongs to her."

The tributes formerly paid by the Indians were abolished. The alcabala, an excessive tax on sales, was also suppressed. The introduction of slaves was forbidden. Different branches of the government were organized.

One of the first works of the Junta was to send emissaries to the several provinces of the old captaincy general to invite them to unite with Caracas in the movement. It was the first government of Spanish America to initiate diplomatic missions abroad. Among her envoys we find Simón Bolívar representing Venezuela at London.

Most of the provinces followed the example given by Caracas, but some of them did not take that action, and among these were Coro and Maracaibo, which exercised powerful influence against the movement for liberty. The emissaries who went to Maracaibo were even sent to Porto Rico to be tried there as rebels and were sentenced to prison in that colony.

Among the diplomatic representatives, some were well received and some were ignored. Bolívar was very highly praised by the London authorities, although he could obtain no substantial assistance because of a treaty of alliance then existing between England and Spain. Bolívar worked not only as a diplomat, but he also wrote and published articles of propaganda to acquire friends for the cause he represented, and from the first his influence was felt all over the continent, especially when he was able to give substantial help to the representatives from Buenos Aires, who went to London to secure the alliance and friendship of England.

The attitude of Venezuela was not only generous and conciliatory, but it was even inspired by a great regard for Spain. The junta declared itself ready to send help to Spain in her fight against the intruder, and also offered the Venezuelan soil as a refuge for those who might despair of the salvation and freedom of the mother country. The Council of Regency which had been established in Spain, instead of thanking Venezuela for her offer, declared the Venezuelans insurgents, rebels and traitors, and submitted the province of Caracas to a strict blockade. This decision on the part of the Council served to arouse the Venezuelans and to change the ends of the movement. The sea became infested with privateers and pirates and, within the country, royalist agencies promoted war and insurrection. Towns which had declared themselves in favor of the Junta were destroyed by the royalists, and everywhere the situation was very difficult for all who had expressed any sympathy with the new régime. Nevertheless, the new authorities persevered in their purpose to show loyalty to Fernando VII, and tried by all means to avoid bloodshed. Even with regard to the governors of Coro and Maracaibo, Caracas tried persuasion rather than force. The uncompromising attitude of the Regency, however, indicated clearly that the Venezuelans could not expect to effect any agreement with Spain. Bolívar, thinking that he could be more useful in his own country than in London, decided to return to Venezuela, but he did not go back alone. We have mentioned before that General Miranda was then living in London. Bolívar invited him to return to Venezuela to help the cause of freedom, for he deemed him the ablest man to lead the movement. He gave him the hospitality of his own home and praised him generously, increasing his popularity.

Miranda was very well received, and the Junta at once appointed him Lieutenant General. At that time the Venezuelans were electing representatives to Congress, and Miranda was elected deputy from one of the cities of the East. Congress entered into session March 2nd with forty-four members, representing seven provinces, and its very first decision was to appoint three men to exercise the executive power and a council to sit for purposes of consultation. Thus the first autonomous government in Latin America was established.

There were several factors active in the creation of public opinion: the press was free, and popular orators held meetings in which they spoke of the new ideas and tried to prepare the people for the new institutions. Special mention should be made of the Sociedad Patriótica (Patriotic Society) whose promoters and leaders were Miranda and Bolívar. This association worked constantly for absolute freedom, putting forward as an example the independence of the North American colonies. Some representatives distrusted the association, considering it as a rival of Congress, but Bolívar relieved their fears by an inspired address delivered on July 3, 1811, which might be considered as the beginning of his career as a great orator. He denounced the apathy of the deputies, denied that there were two congresses, and among other things said:

> "What do we care if Spain submits to Napoleon Bonaparte, if we have decided to be free? Let us without fear lay the corner-stone of South American freedom. To hesitate is to die."

Obeying these feelings, the association sent a memorandum to Congress, which was read on July 4, 1811. The following day this assembly proclaimed the independence of Venezuela. The document contained an exposition of the wrongs suffered by the colony, a decision to live and to die free, and the pledge of seven provinces to sacrifice the lives and fortunes of their inhabitants in this great work. On that same day the national flag of Venezuela was adopted, one containing three horizontal stripes: yellow, blue and red.

Up to this time the revolution had been peaceful and bloodless, but now the royalists of Valencia, a very important city to the west of Caracas, rebelled against the new institutions and asked help from the governors of Coro and Maracaibo. Miranda besieged and took the city, Bolívar fighting on his side. Insurrections broke out in other places and were speedily repressed. In some cities the new state of affairs was welcomed with great joy. The obvious political needs became the object of study of the new Congress. From the beginning the federal system and the central system appeared in opposition. Bolívar was opposed to the federation, arguing that the people of Venezuela were still ignorant and unable to understand the obligations of a federation. At last the partisans of the federation movement were victorious, and Venezuela adopted a federal constitution, in which the most advanced principles with regard to individual rights were incorporated. The epoch of independence was to be called the Colombian epoch, and the first country to free itself from the bond of Spain was to be called Colombia. Colombia (from the name of Columbus) was an ideal of the South American patriots, and the greatest apostle of this ideal was Bolívar, as will be readily seen by this study. Valencia was selected as the capital, and in this city the government established itself on March 1, 1812.

The work of organizing the new government did not interrupt the royalist activity in Venezuela nor the preparations made by Spain to suppress the revolution. The East and the Orinoco valley were in constant agitation, and we have seen that in the West, Coro and Maracaibo were on the side of Spain, and their governors ready to send help to the enemies of independence. Domingo Monteverde, a Spanish naval officer, had arrived in Coro as a member of a Spanish contingent, and when the governor learned that a royalist conspiracy was being prepared in a town called Siquisique, he organized an expedition and gave command of the troops to Monteverde, with instructions to help the conspirators. At that place more men joined his troops. Transgressing the orders he had received, which were only to occupy the town, Monteverde constituted himself head of the army and advanced to fight the insurgents. Luck was undeservedly on his side. On March 23, 1812, he defeated a small body of patriots.

The news of this defeat added to the effect of a natural catastrophe, which came directly on the heels of it, and which was painted by the fanatic royalists as a punishment of Heaven for the uprising. In the afternoon of March 26, at a moment when the churches were filled with people, for it was Holy Thursday, there occurred a violent earthquake in Venezuela. Caracas, La Guaira and many other towns were reduced to ruins, and some small dwellings entirely disappeared. It was pointed out that the towns punished by the earthquake were those that had shown themselves as favoring independence. Whole bodies of troops were buried. In a church of Caracas, the coat-of-arms of Spain had been painted on one of the pillars, and the earthquake destroyed the whole building with the exception of that one pillar. Orators went out into the streets to proclaim that this was unmistakably the result of divine anger because of the rebellion of the people against Fernando VII, "the anointed of God."

In this cataclysm, Bolívar distinguished himself in Caracas, going hither and thither among the ruins, counteracting with his words the effect of the speeches of the royalists and assisting to dig out of the debris corpses and the wounded, giving the latter first aid.

The advance of Monteverde was substantially helped by this earthquake. Many soldiers of the patriots' army had died in their armories and others on their way to fight the enemy and on parade grounds. All the patriot government had was reduced to practically nothing in a moment. Monteverde continued to advance eastward, and took the important town of Barquisimeto, where he received a large contingent of men, who flocked to him fearful of the divine anger. His lieutenants were meeting with success in different fields and he himself soon entered the city of San Carlos.

On the 4th of April, there occurred a second earthquake which lasted eight hours, and which destroyed the little remaining courage of those who were not heart and soul with the movement of emancipation.

* * * *

In the midst of these difficulties, the executive power appointed General Francisco Miranda supreme commander of all the forces of the Republic, on land and sea, and the government withdrew from Valencia to the town of La Victoria, situated between Valencia and Caracas. Miranda went to Caracas to obtain some resources, and while there associated Bolívar with him in the army. Later, Miranda sent him to Puerto Cabello, while Monteverde seized Valencia, the capital of the country.

Various events continued to favor Monteverde, and when Miranda came back to besiege Valencia, Monteverde was so successful that the independent military commander saw himself forced to take a defensive attitude instead of an offensive one. From that moment, Miranda committed error after error, all of which resulted in victories for the fortunate Spanish leader. The patriots grew distrustful of their chief, who withdrew to La Victoria. There he was attacked by Monteverde, but defeated him. This victory availed the patriots little, for Miranda did not want to abandon his defensive position. He had 12,000 men and could have destroyed his enemy, but he preferred to wait. Meanwhile, Bolívar was requesting help to defend Puerto Cabello, where there were deposited many provisions, and also to attack Monteverde by the rear. Miranda refused assistance. Monteverde, upon being defeated in a second attack on La Victoria, withdrew in the direction of Puerto Cabello. Already one of the forts had hoisted the Spanish flag. Monteverde was successful, and Bolívar sailed for La Guaira. The loss of Puerto Cabello, and other facts which need not be mentioned here, decided Miranda to capitulate, at a time when he was still stronger than his enemy. The capitulation was ratified in La Victoria by Miranda on the 25th of July, 1812. The following day Monteverde occupied the city and on the 30th he entered Caracas.

All the patriots denounced Miranda for the capitulation, which meant the dissolution of the army and the abandonment of all the elements which had so raised their hopes.

Bolívar, who, ignorant of the capitulation, had arrived in Caracas on his way to join Miranda, decided to return to La Guaira and to emigrate, resolved never to submit to the Spanish rule. Before departing, he issued a proclamation denouncing emphatically the action of Miranda, and the conduct of Monteverde who had transgressed the laws of war by encouraging the barbarous actions of the undisciplined crowds which, in the interior of the country, were committing all kinds of atrocities. Monteverde had also violated the articles of the capitulation stipulating that the lives and properties of the inhabitants should be respected and that there should follow a general oblivion of all past actions.

Bolívar was in La Guaira when Miranda arrived there with many other officers who were escaping persecution from Monteverde. The generalissimo intended to remain in La Guaira that night, sailing from there the following day. That evening the most prominent men of the city assembled and denounced the supreme commander for his conduct. Among the most bitter judges of Miranda was Bolívar, the man who had asked the London exile to return to Venezuela to work for liberty in his country. The word treachery was uttered and all agreed to imprison Miranda, a culpable action performed on the morning of July 31. That same day the port of La Guaira was closed by order of Monteverde, and the most distinguished patriots who fell into his hands were sent to prison, and cruel persecutions were exercised everywhere. A committee of public safety was established and immediately the prisons of Caracas and Puerto Cabello were filled with men, many of whom died of suffocation. Into a dungeon in Puerto Cabello, a Spaniard threw five flasks of alkali, thus causing the death by asphyxiation of all the prisoners locked there.

The properties of the leading citizens were seized. It was enough to have means of comfortable livelihood to be denounced as an enemy of Spain. The most peaceful men were dragged from their homes, and the tears of wives and children never moved to pity Monteverde's agents.

Miranda, a prisoner in Puerto Cabello, appealed in vain to the audiencia against these crimes. From Puerto Cabello he was sent to Porto Rico and finally to Cádiz, where he was locked in a fortress called la Carraca. There he died on July 14, 1816, his remains being thrown with the corpses of common criminals. Such was the end of the noble man who had been the guest of Catherine II of Russia, a soldier of Washington and a general of the French Republic. He spent his last days in a dungeon, chained to the wall like a dog. Venezuela has erected in the Pantheon of Caracas a beautiful marble monument in the shape of a coffin, the cover of which is held open by the claws of a majestic eagle, waiting for the remains of the great Venezuelan, who committed errors, it is true, but whose devotion to his country has never been doubted and whose martyrdom, and the fortitude with which he bore it, place him among the noblest characters of history.

Bolívar remained in La Guaira for a short while, but inactivity was distasteful. Through the efforts of a Spanish friend, he obtained a passport from Monteverde and left the port for Curaçao at the end of August.

This action marks the end of the first part of Bolívar's life, his restless youth, the preparation for struggles through sorrow and patient study, his military training under Miranda, and the clarification in his mind of the supreme purposes to which he was going to devote his life, no longer in a secondary position, but as a leader, a commanding figure on the American continent.

CHAPTER IV

1812-1813: BOLÍVAR'S FIRST EXPEDITION. THE CRUELTY OF WAR.

After the entrance of Monteverde in Caracas and the ensuing persecutions, all Venezuela could be considered as reconquered for Spain, and it seemed that all was lost for the cause of independence. The disobedience of Monteverde, who, as we have remarked before, had no instructions to continue the campaign, had been forgiven and rewarded, for it had been sanctioned by success. Until the end of 1812, Caracas was treated highhandedly and was very cruelly punished for all interest it had manifested in, and all support it had given to, the cause of independence.

Bolívar joined some patriots in Curaçao, where he remained until October in the company of his relative and loyal friend, José Félix Ribas. He then sailed for Cartagena, a city of New Granada which at that time was free from Spain, and offered his service to the Repúblican government of that city. Bolívar was made colonel under a Frenchman called Pedro Labatut.

In Cartagena, Bolívar continued to write, supporting his idea that the only salvation for the colonies lay in war with Spain. At the end of that year he published a memorandum of so great importance that it can be considered as the first real revelation of his true genius. He explained the reasons for the defeat of Venezuela, and set them forth as a lesson of the urgent need of unity and firmness on the part of the American colonies. He denounced the weakness of the first government, evidenced in the treatment accorded Coro, which was not conquered immediately, but was permitted to be fortified so as to defy the whole federation and finally to destroy it. Recognizing the lack of friendly public opinion, he denounced the junta for not being ready to free the "stupid peoples who do not know the value of their rights."

> "The codes consulted by our magistrates," he wrote, "were not those which could teach them the practical science of government, but those formed by certain idealists who build republics in the air and try to obtain political perfection, presupposing the perfection of the human race, in such a way that we have philosophers as leaders, philanthropy instead of law, dialectic instead of tactics, and sophists instead of soldiers. With this subversion of things, social order was shaken up, and from its very beginning advanced with rapid strides towards universal dissolution, which very soon was effected."

He emphasized the necessity for regular soldiers, trained to fight and experienced enough to know that a single defeat does not mean the loss of all hope, and that "ability and constancy correct misfortune." He denounced the misuse of public funds and declared himself against state paper money not guaranteed, pointing out that such a currency was a clear violation of the right of property, since men who had objects of real value had to exchange them for paper, the price of which was uncertain and even imaginary. Acknowledging that the federal system was the best, he declared that it was the most inadequate for the good of the new states. He added that,

> "as yet our fellow citizens are not in a condition fully to exercise their rights, for they lack the political virtues which characterise a true republic, and which cannot be acquired under an absolute government where the rights and obligations of citizens are ignored."

In another part he said,

> "It is necessary that the government identify itself, so to speak, with the circumstances, times and men surrounding it. If they are prosperous and calm, the government must be mild and protective, but if they are calamitous and turbulent, the government must show itself terrible and must arm itself with a firmness equal to the dangers, without paying heed to laws or constitution, until peace is reestablished."

Bolívar well understood the character of his people when he declared

> "Public elections performed by the ignorant peasants and by the intriguing inhabitants of the city are an obstacle to the practice of federation among us, because the former are so ignorant that they vote like machines, and the latter are so ambitious that they make everything into factions. For these reasons Venezuela has never known a free and reasonable election and the government has fallen into the hands of men, either opposed to the cause, weak or immoral. Partisan spirit decided everything and, consequently, it disorganized us more than circumstances did. Our divisions, and not the Spanish Army, brought us back to slavery."

Summarizing the causes of the fall of Venezuela, he attributed it in the first place to the nature of its constitution; secondly, to the discouragement of the government and people; thirdly, to the opposition to the establishment of a regular military organization; fourthly, to earthquakes and superstitions strengthened by those calamities, and fifthly and lastly to

> "the internal dissensions, which, in fact, were the deadly poison which carried the country to its doom."

Then he appealed with persuasive eloquence to Nueva Granada for help, arguing that it was indispensable for Nueva Granada to reobtain the freedom of Caracas, pointing out that as Coro, as an enemy, had been enough to destroy the whole of Venezuela, so Venezuela as a center of Spanish power would suffice to recover Nueva Granada for the Spanish crown. The possession of Caracas by Spain was a danger for all Spanish America. Then he showed the possibility of a military undertaking, starting from Nueva Granada, and expressed his faith that thousands of valiant patriots would join the ranks of the army of liberty as soon as it set foot in Venezuela. He gave the details of the proposed campaign, and finished with a most eloquent and forceful appeal in the following words:

> "The honor of Nueva Granada imperatively requires the punishment of the daring invaders, their persecution to the last trenches. Her glory will be the undertaking of going to Venezuela, and freeing the birthplace of Colombian independence and its martyrs, and that worthy people of Caracas, whose clamors are addressed to their beloved fellow patriots of Nueva Granada, for whom they are waiting with deadly impatience as for their redeemers. Let us hasten to break the chains of those victims who moan in the dungeons, ever expecting their salvation from you. Do not betray their confidence, do not be heedless of the lamentations of your brothers. Be eager to avenge the dead, to bring back to life the dying, to relieve the oppressed and to give liberty to all."

This noteworthy document was published in Cartagena, on December 15, 1812, and presents Bolívar as he was in the maturity of his life, as a thinker, apostle, general, and practical statesman; it shows him as the man destined to give liberty to five countries. This proclamation is the first full display of Bolívar's genius.

Bolívar was sent to command a small place where he had to be inactive. He prepared an expedition against the city of Tenerife, considered one of the strongest in Nueva Granada and which prevented the free navigation of the Magdalena River. He left with only 400 men and seized the castle abandoned by the garrison, thus obtaining some artillery, boats and war material. Following his success, the government of Cartagena placed him in full command of his own army and gave him orders to conquer the upper Magdalena. Bolívar accomplished this with only 500 men, freeing the east bank of the river. When he arrived at Ocaña, he was received amidst the greatest enthusiasm. He had won five victories in five days.

The Congress of Nueva Granada was holding its meetings in the city of Tunja. Bolívar got in touch with it and received instructions to lead an expedition against Cúcuta and Pamplona. He started out with 400 men and a few spare rifles to arm patriots who might join the ranks. With the greatest alacrity he advanced, defeating several detachments on the way. He finally attacked the city of Cúcuta, where 800 royalists were awaiting the attack of his men. On the 28th of February, after a bloody fight, Bolívar took the city and considerably increased his supply of war implements. The royalists occupying Pamplona and neighboring towns evacuated their possessions upon learning of the defeat of the royalists of Cúcuta. On sending communications to the governor of Cartagena, Bolívar dated them in the city of "Cúcuta delivered" (libertada). His habit of adding the word "libertada" to the cities captured from the royalists contributed greatly to his later receiving the name of "Libertador," by which he is most generally known in history.

As soon as he entered Venezuelan territory, he declared that on that very day Venezuela had returned to life. Addressing the soldiers, he said:

> "In less than two months you have carried out two campaigns and have begun a third one, which commences here and which must end in the country which gave me life."

He regarded his two previous campaigns merely as an introduction to the third, and most important for him, whose supreme ambition was to obtain once again the freedom of Venezuela. At the close of the address to the soldiers, we find these words:

> "All America expects its liberty and salvation from you, brave soldiers of Cartagena and of the Union." (The Union of Nueva Granada.)

These words indicate that he was thinking not in local terms, but in terms of Greater America.

The government of the Union promoted him to the rank of brigadier general and conferred upon him the honorary title of citizen of Nueva Granada. He asked immediate authority to use the troops of the Union to continue his march, until he could recover the ruins of Caracas. To convince the government he repeated the arguments put forth in the proclamation of Cartagena, tending to prove that the freedom of Venezuela was essential to the continued liberty of Nueva Granada. He insisted so eloquently on receiving permission to advance, that at last he obtained it, with authorization to occupy the southwestern provinces of Venezuela: Mérida and Trujillo. In thanking the executive power for this privilege, he evidenced his confidence in his future triumph by the following words, addressed to the president:

> "I ask Your Excellency to send the answer to this communication to Trujillo: I shall receive it there."

Bolívar started his campaign from San Cristóbal on the 15th of May, 1813, with 800 men. The royalists had 15,000 and sufficient resources to equip 6,000 additional men. The work of the young warrior seemed a dream; perhaps no wise general would have undertaken that campaign, but Bolívar was above common wisdom; he had the power of making the most beautiful dreams come true. Among the men who accompanied him were many who have received the greatest honors history can confer. Two of them may be noted here, for we shall have occasion to mention them again very soon; they are Atanasio Girardot and Antonio Ricaurte.

Upon his approach to Mérida, the royalists, numbering 1,000, left the city, and Bolívar took it on the 30th of May without any opposition. He was received with enthusiasm as the liberator of Venezuela. The general began at once to attend to the organization of the emancipated territory, and to increase the strength of his army. He sent some men to attack the retreating Spaniards, and Girardot to occupy the province of Trujillo. The royalists escaped to Maracaibo and, on the 14th of June, Bolívar was in Trujillo, reorganizing the province. From there he sent Girardot to pursue the royalists.

On the next day Bolívar took an action which has been the subject of many debates, and which some writers consider is the one stain in the career of the great man of the South. We must devote a few lines to frank discussion of this subject, not neglecting to declare immediately that in our minds there has never been the slightest doubt that Bolívar was right in his conduct, and that a different action would have been the height of folly. Bolívar proclaimed "War to Death to the Spaniards," considering the conduct of Monteverde, the savage crimes committed in the interior cities of Venezuela, the many instances in which the Spanish authorities had shown an utter disrespect for the sanctity of treaties and the lives and properties of enemies who had surrendered, and even of peaceful natives, these acts coupled with documents like the proclamation published by a Spanish governor of a province in which he stated that his troops would not give quarter to those who surrendered. The documents proving that this proclamation had been issued were received by Bolívar in Trujillo. In Bolívar's mind this idea was a permanent obsession: "Americans are dying because they are Americans, whether or not they fight for American freedom." He took into account the long list of crimes committed, the harmless citizens, women and children who had died, the barbarous asphyxiation of the prisoners in Puerto Cabello, the horrors committed on the peaceful inhabitants of Caracas, and even the atrocities perpetrated by the royalist armies in Mexico and other parts of the continent.

He recalled the leniency and mercy of the first independent government of Venezuela and the cruelty of the Spanish authorities, and thought, not only of the reprisals necessary to punish and, if possible, to stop these cruel deeds, but also of the salutary effect of a rigorous attitude on hesitating men, and the necessity that those who had not taken part on one side or another should declare themselves immediately, whether they sympathized with and were ready to help the cause of liberty, or favored a foreign régime. He was still in Mérida when in a proclamation he spoke of avenging the victims, and threatened with war to death. But Bolívar was not only a man of genius but one of equanimity, poise, deep thought and attention. He did not want to carry out his threats immediately, but decided to think at length over the transcendent step he was considering. The night of the 14th of June was a night of torture for the Liberator. On the morning of the 15th he himself wrote the decree of *War to Death*, and then called for an assembly of his officers to hear their opinions of this decree. Not one of them dissented. At the close of the meeting Bolívar signed the proclamation, in which these terrible words appeared:

> "Spaniards and Natives of the Canary Islands:[4] Be sure of death even if you are indifferent. Americans: Be sure of life even if you are guilty."

The law of war is a terrible law, and Bolívar could not but take this step, unless he preferred to wage a losing fight.

As a measure of legitimate reprisal and as a measure of wisdom in warfare, the War to Death decree is fully justifiable.

Regarding it as a reprisal, let us mention only two or three facts. When Monteverde learned of the asphyxiation of the prisoners in Puerto Cabello, he wrote to the commander of the port:

> "I strongly recommend that your activity on this point be not slackened (the expulsion of foreigners from Puerto Cabello), nor on that of the safe-keeping of the prisoners in the dungeons. If any one is to die, that is his fate."

On the plains some towns were entirely destroyed by bands of assassins. Women and children were the victims of the royalists in a number of cities. There were occasions where men and women of all ages had their ears cut off, were skinned alive, or in other ways cruelly tortured. A Spaniard called Boves distinguished himself among the worst criminals. He systematically organized the work of destroying Americans. His theory was that no American should live, and he simply destroyed them mechanically, for he thought that that was the only thing to do with them.

---

4 Many of the natives of the Canary Islands had distinguished themselves by their cruelty against the independents in Venezuela.

Bolívar, himself, in a letter sent to the governor of Curaçao on October 2, 1813, makes the most eloquent exposition of facts, and shows clearly the reasons he had for the decree of War to Death.

Still, Bolívar did not carry out the decree of War to Death immediately, nor did he do so constantly. Whenever he found any opportunity to exercise mercy, he did so; and when he was forced to let the severity of this law fall upon his enemy, there was generally an immediate reason for his action. In San Carlos, a few days after the issuance of this decree, when addressing the Spaniards and the Natives of the Canary Islands, he said:

> "For the last time, Spaniards and Natives of the Canary Islands, listen to the voice of justice and clemency. If you prefer our cause to that of tyrants, you will be forgiven and will enjoy your property, and honor; but if you persist in being our enemies, withdraw from our country or prepare to die."

Several proofs are recorded of his clemency in spite of his threats; but at last, when he saw that there was no other way to bring the royalists to terms, he ordered that war be waged mercilessly.

CHAPTER V

1813: BOLÍVAR'S FIRST VICTORIES.

The Congress of Nueva Granada had ordered Bolívar to take Trujillo and there to await new instructions. It was reluctant to permit him to advance, because the patriots in Nueva Granada found themselves in a difficult position. Bolívar wrote them, showing the necessity of his advancing immediately, in order to prevent the enemy from discovering the reduced size of his army and destroying it. His plan was to advance steadily against the royalists, to destroy them, and thus secure the freedom of Nueva Granada. Finally, the Congress yielded.

Bolívar's situation was an exceedingly dangerous one. There was a good-sized royalist army to his right, while to his left were the old hostile cities of Maracaibo and Coro. Before him was Monteverde with the men who had helped him to conquer Venezuela and with an abundant supply of war material. He became so impatient that he advanced without having received an answer to his last communication to Congress, crossed the Andes and, on the first of July, took the city of Guanare. Meanwhile, General Ribas, following Bolívar's orders, also advanced, meeting a detachment of royalists sent to cut off Bolívar's retreat. Ribas had less than half as many men as his opponent, but he was a man of the stamp of his leader, and on the same day that Bolívar entered Guanare he attacked the enemy. When his limited supply of ammunition was exhausted, he fought with the bayonet, and succeeded in completely destroying his foes. This battle occurred in a town called Niquitao, and is considered one of the most brilliant battles of the War of Independence.

Bolívar continued his rapid advance to the city of Barinas, and found it

abandoned by the royalists, who had left behind artillery and ammunition. He ordered his trusted Girardot to continue the prosecution of the enemy, but they made their escape towards Venezuelan Guiana (Guayana) by means of one of the tributaries of the Orinoco, leaving behind them a path marked with crimes and depredations.

Once in possession of Barinas, Bolívar reorganized the province, created his first troops of cavalry, instilled enthusiasm in the population and prepared himself for new steps in his brilliant career. To Ribas, he entrusted the defeat of some 1,500 royalists whose position might hinder his progress. With only one-third this number of men, Ribas encountered and destroyed the enemy on the plains of Los Horcones, which victory, together with that at Niquitao, did much for the success of the whole campaign.

Leaving a detachment in Barinas, Bolívar advanced to San Carlos, which he entered on the 28th of July, and then continued onward towards Valencia.

While Bolívar was advancing from the western border towards the heart of his country, very important events were taking place in the eastern extremity. A young man named don Diego Mariño, after having made preparations in the Island of Trinidad to fight against the Spanish domination in his country, entered Venezuela and advanced to the city of Cumaná. There is a striking similarity in the lives and labors of Bolívar and Mariño. Both were young, both were animated by the same hatred of tyranny and the same love for independence; both knew how to arouse enthusiasm in their followers and both displayed the greatest devotion to their friends; both were inspired by the same ambition for glory and honor, and both realized a very important part of the first liberation of Venezuela.

Monteverde attacked Mariño and met with disaster, being compelled to withdraw to Caracas, where he learned of the victories of Bolívar in the West. He immediately prepared to go personally to Valencia to stop the advance of the independents. There he was informed of the latest triumph of Ribas.

Bolívar advanced, destroyed in Taguanes a strong army sent to check him, and continued his march toward Valencia, prepared to meet a strong resistance on the part of Monteverde. Great indeed was his surprise when he found that Monteverde had escaped toward Puerto Cabello during the night, leaving everything to the mercy of the conqueror.

From Valencia, the victor went to Caracas, where he granted an honorable capitulation to the city, offering passports to the Spanish soldiers and officers and permitting them to evacuate the town in the most dignified way. Upon his arrival in Caracas, Bolívar. found that soldiers and officers, as well as about six thousand persons who considered themselves guilty, had already escaped to La Guaira, confident that Bolívar would act as Monteverde had done in the past.

August 6th, 1813, marks the entrance of Bolívar in Caracas, the end of the campaign which he had begun with 500 men,—his first campaign as a general, one in which he fought six pitched battles, covered a distance of 1,200 kilometers, destroyed five hostile armies, captured 50 pieces of artillery and three ammunition depots, and reconquered all the western part of Venezuela, while Eastern Venezuela had been recovered by Mariño. All this was done within ninety days, and established forever the reputation of Bolívar as one of the most distinguished generals in history.

Caracas received him with the highest honors. The most beautiful young ladies of the city, dressed in white, brought flowers and branches of laurel to the conqueror; church bells were rung; flowers were strewn in his path. Bolívar, with his usual energy, set to work at once to reestablish order and to arrange to continue operations against La Guaira. He issued a proclamation announcing the rebirth of the Republic, and expressing his gratitude to Nueva Granada, to whom Venezuela owed the beginning of this undertaking. In order to avoid the necessity of fulfilling his decree of War to Death, he sent messengers to Puerto Cabello to ask Monteverde to ratify the convention by which he granted life to all Spaniards caught in Caracas or on their way to La Guaira, but Monteverde refused, explaining that he did not want to have any dealings with the insurgents.

As soon as the most urgent work of organization was finished, Bolívar, who had sent cordial congratulations to Mariño, went himself to conduct the siege of Puerto Cabello.

At that period, when his glory was at its greatest splendor, he made the first public declaration by which the world could know that he had no personal ambition. He, who in his youth had enjoyed all the comforts and pleasures of life; who had had, in various parts of Venezuela, vast estates, slaves which he had set free, and all kinds of personal possessions; and who had abandoned everything to devote his life to his efforts in the service of his country, said these words:

> "The Liberator of Venezuela renounces forever and declines irrevocably to accept any office except the post of danger at the head of our soldiers in defense of the salvation of our country."

And Bolívar lived up to his words.

Monteverde held many patriots in Puerto Cabello. Bolívar proposed an exchange of prisoners, but the Spaniard steadily refused all reasonable demands. The siege of Puerto Cabello was not altogether successful because the city was open to the sea and the royalist army was able to receive provisions. A strong expedition commanded by don José Miguel Salomón arrived from Spain to help Monteverde, and Bolívar realized that he could not hope to succeed unless the enemy could be drawn out of the city to fight in the open. Consequently, he ordered his troops to withdraw. Monteverde came out of the city on the 30th of September, and was attacked by three independent columns which defeated him completely. They themselves suffered a distressing loss in the death of Colonel Girardot, who was killed by a bullet in the forehead while hoisting in a captured position the flag of independence. Bolívar paid the greatest honor to Girardot, and took the heart of his young lieutenant to Caracas to receive the homage of the people. The soldiers and followers of Girardot asked Bolívar the privilege of being sent to avenge the young colonel. Monteverde had established himself in a place which he considered impregnable. The insurgents attacked with all their might, and the enemy was routed. Monteverde had to withdraw to Puerto Cabello, where he was deposed by his subordinates and Salomón was elected to take his place. His successor accepted the exchange of prisoners, and Bolívar, leaving some troops to continue the siege of the port, went to Caracas, where he had to face new difficulties.

The communication with Nueva Granada had been cut by the Spanish troops sent from Maracaibo. In Cúcuta the royalists were committing all kinds of brutal deeds. It is said that assassinations were committed as the result of bets. Children under ten years of age had their hands cut off. In the Orinoco plains, the *llanos*, Boves with his lieutenant, Morales, exceeded whatever imagination can fancy in the way of bloodthirsty cruelty. Some independent detachments had been destroyed in the South, and several fanatical priests were discouraging sympathizers of freedom, declaring that "The King is the representative of God."[5]

Bolívar sent Brigadier General Urdaneta, who had distinguished himself in the previous campaigns, to take charge of the army of the West. Campo-Elías, another trusted officer, was sent to the plains, while Bolívar himself went to Caracas to pay his last homage to the heart of Girardot, an action by which he not only honored his dead officer, but also showed his appreciation of the help received from Nueva Granada in the work of securing the independence of his country. In Caracas,

5 It is necessary, at this point, to make very plain the attitude of the Catholic clergy in the wars of American independence. Of course, no man of good sense and culture will today pay any attention to the accusations against Spain, the clergy and the Inquisition, all inspired by religious hatred, which is one of the worst forms of fanaticism. Nevertheless, there are still fanatics who refuse to open their eyes to the truth, either because they find their ignorance a very comfortable frame of mind or because they maliciously devote themselves to the abominable work of slandering a country and institutions which have played and are playing a very important historical rôle.

There appears to be only one serious monograph on Simón Bolívar written in English, and this is an article which appeared in Harper's New Monthly Magazine, No. 238, V. 40, published in March, 1870. This article was written by Eugene Lawrence, and pretends to be a eulogy of the Man of the South. In substance it is nothing more than a superficial synopsis of the main facts of the public life of Bolívar, and a constant and virulent attack against Spain and the Catholic Church. It would seem that to the author Spain is nothing, and has never been anything, but kings and priests, and that kings and priests are a curse on the population. The cruelties of the Spanish kings and priests constitute his main subject. As a matter of fact, in the political revolutions of America, the priests have been divided and have acted like other men, availing themselves of their right to their own opinions. The greatest proof that the Church is not to take any blame or praise for whatever happened in the War of Independence is that it did not force its dignitaries to take any particular stand. They did as they pleased. There were priests on the side of Monteverde and there were priests on the side of Bolívar. Undoubtedly, the former thought and preached that the will of God was to keep the American countries in subjection, while the latter might have believed that the independence of the American countries would satisfy the desires of God. If the Church was on the side of Spain, the Spaniards certainly failed to reward her. In a letter to the Governor of Curaçao, Bolívar wrote: "Many respectable old men, many venerable priests, have seen themselves in chains and in other infamous ways prisoners, herded with common criminals and men of the lowest stamp, exposed to the insults of brutal soldiers and of the vilest men of the lowest station." On the other hand, several priests accompanied Bolívar, and he always showed the greatest veneration for the Church and for its members. Speaking, then, of priests exploiting the fanaticism of the crowd, no sober-minded historian would ever intend an attack against the Church in general. Furthermore, we must not forget that most of the enemies of independence were Americans, and that some publicists refuse to speak of it as a war of independence but term the revolution a civil war.

Bolívar for the first time received officially the name of "Savior of the Country, Liberator of Venezuela." On receiving the decree conferring these titles upon him, he said that the title of Liberator of Venezuela was more glorious and satisfying to him than the crowns of all the empires of the world, but that the real liberators had been the Congress of Nueva Granada, Ribas, Girardot and the other men who had been with him throughout the campaign.

Bolívar was very much concerned with the increasing wave of discontent which threatened to destroy his work. As we said at the beginning, there was no public opinion to support him. The masses were moved by their feelings, by early acquired habits, by superstitions or by low interests, and the *llaneros* (inhabitants of the plains) would follow any chieftain who could guarantee them sufficient loot. At only thirty years of age Bolívar had proved himself as great a statesman as he was a soldier. He arranged for the organization of all public services, and when this was attended to, he took care to satisfy the natural pride of the patriots, by creating an order called "The Military Order of the Liberators of Venezuela."

CHAPTER VI

1813-1814: ARAURE. RIBAS TRIUMPHS IN LA VICTORIA. A WHOLESALE EXECUTION.

The Governor of Coro had come out of the city with 1,300 men and had destroyed an independent army. He now threatened the possession of Valencia and the security of the troops engaged in the siege of Puerto Cabello. Yáñez, at the head of 2,500 *llaneros*, had destroyed another patriot army and had seized the city of Barinas, leaving his path strewn with corpses and stained with the blood of his victims.

Urdaneta sent news of his danger to the Liberator, and the latter came at once to the rescue, and defeated in Barquisimeto the army of Coro, only to see this victory turned to defeat as the result of a mistaken bugle order which caused the retreat of one of his regiments. Urdaneta was entrusted with the organization of the remains of the patriotic army, and Bolívar went to Valencia to obtain new reinforcements. The Governor of Coro, D. José Ceballos by name, succeeded in getting in touch with Yáñez and the Governor of Puerto Cabello, and concerted a combined attack. Bolívar ordered Ribas, who was at that time in Caracas, to come to the rescue with all the men he could gather. The commander of Puerto Cabello, Salomón, advancing on the road which leads from Valencia to Caracas, was attacked by Ribas and by Bolívar and, after three days of constant fighting, was forced to withdraw to the port, having suffered very heavy losses. Then Bolívar, with all the men that he could summon, proceeded to San Carlos, where he found himself with 3,000 armed men ready to fight the royalists. With this army he advanced to meet Ceballos, and met him, commanding 3,500 men, near a place called Araure. The great battle of Araure was fought on the 5th of December, 1813. At first it was costly to the insurgent armies, which lost their best infantrymen. But the Liberator was present everywhere, encouraging his soldiers and directing their movements. At last, the independents obtained the victory, and the royalists had to withdraw, leaving 1,000 dead and many guns. After that battle, Ceballos and Yáñez had to escape to the south, to the valley of the Orinocó. Bolívar's prestige was shown at its best.

The regiment which, through a mistake, had begun the retreat at the battle of Barquisimeto, Bolívar punished by depriving it of the right to have a flag and a name until it would conquer them in the field of battle. The "Nameless Battalion" was placed in the center of the independent forces in Araure, and ten minutes after the battle had started, it had conquered a flag from the enemy and had broken through the royalist army.

From that date the "Nameless Battalion" was called "The Conqueror of Araure."

The victory at Araure destroyed in one day the armies oppressing Venezuela, and was the last military triumph of 1813, a year of success for the independent army.

On thanking his staff for the congratulations which they addressed to him, Bolívar uttered the following significant words:

> "It is true that our armies have avenged Venezuela. The largest army which has tried to subjugate us lies destroyed on the field. But we cannot rest. Other obligations await us. And when our native is entirely free, we shall go to fight the Spaniards in any part of America where they are in control, and we shall throw them into the sea. Freedom shall live protected by our swords."

But Bolívar's concern was increasing. He well knew that he was not supported by public opinion, and he was also aware that the cruel crowds of the plains were his greatest menace.

He sent a communication to the Congress of Nueva Granada, notifying it of the conquest of the West and of his preparation for war against the men of the plains, explaining again his attitude with regard to personal power.

> "The possession of supreme authority," he wrote, "so flattering for the despots of the other continent, has been for me, the lover of liberty, heavy and displeasing."

In another he added:

> "I shall not retain any part of the authority, even if the people themselves would entrust it to me."

His report of the 31st of December is one of the most conspicuous documents of the life of Bolívar. It ranks as high as his proclamation of Cartagena at the beginning of the campaign. In this report, through his Secretary of Foreign Relations, he expressed his idea about union between Nueva Granada and Venezuela. The document appears as addressed to him, and of it the following words deserve special consideration:

> "The lessons of experience should not be lost for us. The spectacle presented to us by Europe, steeped in blood in an endeavor to establish a balance which is forever changing, should correct our policy in order to save it from those bloody dangers.... Besides that continental balance of power which Europe is seeking where it seems less likely to be found, that is, through war and disturbances, there is another balance, a balance

which concerns us, the balance of the universe. The ambition of the European countries is to reduce to slavery the other parts of the world, and all these other parts of the world should endeavor to establish a balance between themselves and Europe in order to destroy the preponderance of the latter. I call this the balance of the world, and it must enter into the calculations of American policies.

"It is necessary that our country be sufficiently strong to resist successfully the aggressions which European ambitions may plan; and this colossal power, which must oppose another great power, cannot be formed but through the union of all South America under a national body, so that a single government may use its great resources a single purpose, that of resisting with all of them exterior aggressions, while in the interior an increasing mutual cooperation of all will lift us to the summit of power and prosperity."

The present ideas of inter-American coöperation do not differ very much from those existing in the mind of Bolívar.

Following the deposition of Monteverde, the army of Puerto Cabello had left for Coro and practically disappeared on its way. But some royalists had gone to the south, and entered the city of Calabozo, after having destroyed an insurgent force. Its commander was one of the worst men who had ever breathed the air of America, José Tomás Rodríguez, a native of Spain, who, after having been a pirate, was sentenced to the prison of Puerto Cabello. Several Spaniards applied for a mitigation of the sentence, and he was set free within the city of Calabozo, where he was employed when the revolution began. By that time he had changed his name to that of Boves. He first joined the patriots' army, but for some reason or other he was imprisoned. He was released in 1810 by the royalists, and swore revenge against the revolutionists. He organized a cavalry corps and committed infamous deeds of cruelty wherever he happened to be, at the same time achieving military success for, though morally a beast, he was clever in the field of battle and possessed dauntless bravery. He held the banks of the Orinoco with the aid of his lieutenant, Francisco Tomás Morales, a native of the Canary Islands, whose moral worth can be judged by a single word applied to him by Boves himself. Boves called him "atrocious." While Boves killed Americans systematically, considering that it was the best, and perhaps the only way to end the insurrection, Morales killed Americans for pleasure, whether or not their death would foster the ends of the royalists. He had formerly been a servant. He was brave and obdurate, and a very able second. In the army of Boves, composed of 4,000 *llaneros*, he helped to take the city of Calabozo. Bolívar immediately asked Mariño, who was commanding in the East, to help him, but for several reasons, and perhaps mainly because

Mariño wanted to have supreme power, he did not go to the rescue. This was the sad state of affairs at the beginning of 1814.

This year began with an assembly in Caracas of representatives of the people, to whom Bolívar submitted a report on the use he had made of his authority. On that occasion Bolívar spoke his mind as plainly as before. Although his words depicted legitimate pride, he was very anxious to make it understood that he was unwilling to retain any power over the nation. Among other things he said:

> "I accepted and retained the supreme authority in order to save you from anarchy and to destroy the enemy who tried to support the party of oppression. I have given you laws, I organized for you the administration of justice and revenue, and, finally, I have given you a government.
>
> "Fellow citizens: I am not the sovereign. Your representatives should draw up your laws. The national treasury does not belong to the government. All those who have kept your wealth should show you the use they have made of it.... I am anxious to transfer this power to the representatives you must appoint, and I hope you will relieve me of a burden, which one of you can worthily bear, giving me the only honor to which I aspire, that is, to continue to fight your enemies, for I shall never sheathe my sword until the freedom of my country is altogether secure."

The political governor of Caracas answered the address of the Liberator, praising him for his brilliant campaign and for the successes due to his genius. After a brief summary of his heroic deeds in Nueva Granada, he said that the greatest merit of a man lay in the handing over of the power entrusted to him. To take the power from Bolívar, he reasoned, would very likely work to the ruin of the country, and he expressed his belief that the thing necessary to do was to offer Bolívar supreme power for the time being. In his answer to the governor, Bolívar paid a deserving tribute to his brothers-in-arms, and then added the following words:

> "I have not come to oppress you with my victorious arms. I have come to bring you the empire of law. I have come with the purpose of preserving your sacred rights. It is not military despotism which can make a people free, and the power I have never can be good for the Republic except for a short period. A successful soldier does not acquire any right to command his country. He is not the arbiter of laws and government; he is the defender of freedom, and his glories must be identical to those of the Republic and his ambition satisfied if he gives happiness to his country.... Elect your representatives, your magistrates, a just government, and be sure that the armies which have saved the Republic will always protect the freedom and the national glory of Venezuela."

Nevertheless, in spite of his protestations, the power was forced upon him. He did not stay long in the work of the government, but soon devoted his time to the conduct of war. Puerto Cabello, with fewer soldiers than before, was the main object of his attention. He intended to put an end to the siege, attacking the town at one time by land and by sea. Misunderstandings with Mariño, who had sent some reinforcements previously, prevented the successful carrying out of his plan.

Barinas had fallen into the hands of the royalist Yáñez, whose bloodthirsty followers beheaded eighty soldiers who had been left behind, killed men, women and children, and destroyed the whole city by fire. A few days later this man was killed in a skirmish, and thus ended the life of a fiend whose name may be placed at the side of those of Boves and Morales, because of his delight in committing crimes. In the rest of the country the royalists were conducting guerrilla warfare, preventing the reunion of patriotic bodies and rendering the situation very critical for Bolívar. The largest troops of royalists were generally commanded by men distinguished for their

ferocity. To the names appearing elsewhere we must add those of Calzada, Yáñez' successor, and of Rosete, who competed with each other for the distinction of shedding the most blood.

Boves, in command of the horsemen of the plains, won a great victory in a place called La Puerta, over Campo-Elías, and as a result he reached the valley of Valencia and approached the city of Caracas. The city of Ocumare was taken by Rosete, who proceeded to kill even the persons who were in church praying to God.

In an effort to take advantage of his favorable position by swift movements, Boves advanced to a city called La Victoria, on the road from Valencia to Caracas, where Ribas was ready to do his utmost to prevent the triumph of the bloodthirsty *llaneros*. On the morning of February 12, 1814, Boves attacked and succeeded in entering the town, but he found that the garrison was made up of extraordinary men, one of whom was worth four of his own, thanks to the inspiration and bravery of Ribas. The number of casualties was enormous. Ribas saw his best officers falling about him, and he himself had three horses killed under him. In the middle of the afternoon the result of the battle was still undecided. Then troops gathered by Campo-Elías after his defeat of La Puerta joined the defenders. Ribas pushed out of the city and destroyed whatever appeared in his path. Boves retreated and installed himself on the outskirts. The following day he was attacked again and was forced to withdraw, this time in utter disorder. The battle of La Victoria was the greatest victory of Ribas, and is counted among the most brilliant feats of arms during the Venezuelan War of Independence, filled as it was with heroic deeds.

Bolívar did not fail properly to praise the conqueror. He announced the triumph to Caracas and to the world, and in paying tribute to the living hero, he did not forget to pay homage to those who had fallen on the field of battle. On that occasion, he uttered one of those brilliant expressions so common in his writings: "Ribas, against whom adversity is powerless." ... He never felt that his own glory had to suffer from the unstinted praise he bestowed on his followers.

After this victory at La Victoria, Ribas went to Ocumare, where he saw the work of Rosete, who had left the streets strewn with dying men, women and children, and with the corpses of many victims of his insatiable ferocity. More than 300 had fallen at the hands of the monsters. Bodies and mutilated members appeared everywhere, the best proof of how just had been Bolívar's decree of War to Death. Among other things Ribas found a branding iron in the shape of a *P*, with which Rosete had intended to mark the foreheads of the patriots and those of their children.

Bolívar, who in spite of the frequent atrocities of the enemy, had had his decree carried out very seldom and very reluctantly, now, with the royalists in command of Boves, Rosete and Morales, found it necessary to begin severe reprisals in earnest.

The prisoners taken by the independents were constantly plotting. When Boves was threatening Caracas, the commander of La Guaira asked Bolívar what he was to do with the Spaniards in the prisons of the city, considering that they were numerous and the garrison very small. The Liberator answered as follows:

> "I command you to execute immediately all the Spaniards in the fortress and in the hospital, without exception."

He gave a similar order to the authorities in Caracas. As a result of these orders, 886 Spaniards and natives of the Canary Islands were executed.

This is the act for which Bolívar has been most severely criticised and his conduct most generally condemned. But, if what we have already said is not sufficient to prove the need of these reprisals, we can take into consideration also the slow torture to which the sick independents in the hospital had been subjected, the killing of a woman because she had been accused of having embroidered a uniform for Bolívar, the destruction of the innocent dwellers in the towns taken by the royalists. This decision must be considered also as a measure of safety, for Bolívar could not see an enemy approaching, realizing the necessity perhaps of a hasty retreat, and leave behind him reinforcements for his foes. On this occasion, Bolívar was not merciful, but mercy had been repeatedly exercised by him even against the dictates of wisdom. His measure of reprisal in this case can be considered as ferocious only by contrast with his previous clemency. As a historian (Baralt) remarks:

"It must be agreed that the patience of saints could not tolerate the crimes of the royalist leaders, and at that very moment new attacks increased indignation and anger to an inexpressible degree."

CHAPTER VII

1814: THE HEROIC DEATH OF RICAURTE. VICTORY OF CARABOBO AND DEFEAT OF LA PUERTA.

Boves had retreated from La Victoria, but after reorganizing his army he was again ready to attack. Bolívar had very few men, for the country was nearly exhausted. With them he waited the dreaded royalist in a place called San Mateo, where he was attacked by an army at least four times as large as his. He had but one advantage, having selected a hilly ground where the cavalry of the enemy could not easily maneuver. The battle began on the 28th of February. It lasted all that day, and at the end of ten and one-half hours of constant fighting, Bolívar was master of the situation, not without having lost some of his best men, among them the valiant Campo-Elías, who died a few days later.

Boves, wounded also, withdrew and waited for reinforcements, which arrived in great numbers from the plains; while Bolívar had to reduce the defenders of San Mateo in order to send some men to protect Caracas, which was being threatened on the southeast by Rosete. Boves attacked again on the 20th of March and was once more repulsed. Being informed that Rosete had been defeated at Ocumare by the independents and that Mariño was approaching to the relief of Bolívar, he decided to make a desperate effort to take San Mateo. On the 25th of March he made a third attempt, and that day marks the occurrence of one of the heroic deeds of the ages.

The supplies and the hospital of the insurgents were at a house built on a hill, while the fight developed down below on the farm of San Mateo, owned by Bolívar. Antonio Ricaurte, a native of Santa Fé (Nueva Granada) was in command of the house. Boves decided to take this position and, in the middle of the combat, the independents on the plain discovered that a large column of royalists had stolen towards the ammunition depot from the opposite side of the hill. All felt that the war material was lost. Ricaurte was known as a brave man, but he could do little with the very few men in his command. The young man had the wounded men taken down to the plain, then he ordered his own soldiers to follow, and he remained alone. The enemies continued to advance, and finally entered the house. Suddenly there was heard a terrific explosion, and, when the smoke had cleared, it could be seen that the house had been partially destroyed. Ricaurte had blown up the ammunition, and with it himself and the enemy. Thus Bolívar's army was saved. Boves, who had attacked thirty times, retreated immediately, leaving nearly 1,000 men dead on the field of battle. The loss of the patriots had been as big, or bigger, than that of Boves, but success remained with them. Ricaurte took his place among men who, like Leonidas, deemed life of little value as compared with the salvation of their country.

Further to the west, Ceballos, the former governor of Coro, had obliged the patriots to retreat towards Valencia, where they were besieged by him with reinforcements brought by Boves, who, after his defeat at San Mateo, had fought Mariño, meeting again with disaster. In spite of the reinforcements, the royalists were forced to retreat when the garrison of Valencia was reduced to less than half of its former size.

Mariño and Bolívar met in La Victoria. The former, with an army made up of his men and some given by Bolívar, proceeded to the west to fight against Ceballos, while Bolívar went to Puerto Cabello, intending to take the city by storm. By an imprudent move on his own part, Mariño was forced to meet an army superior to his own, and he was defeated. He then withdrew to Valencia, where Bolívar hastened to meet him, once more leaving the city of Puerto Cabello. There he learned that Ceballos had received reinforcements, and went to Caracas to recruit more men from a city which by now was bled white. Nevertheless, he did obtain a few more men, and these he sent to Valencia under Ribas, following shortly in order to take personal command of the army in the battle.

The contending armies met on a plain called Carabobo, the royalists with many more men than there were patriots. Desertions from the forces of the Repúblicans were frequent. This caused Bolívar much concern, as did the news that Boves was advancing from the south with a great body of cavalry. With Mariño and Ribas to help him, and with his most trusted officers at the head of the different sections, he advanced against the enemy, commanded at that time by the Spanish field-marshal, D. Juan Manuel Cagigal. This first battle of Carabobo, fought on the 28th of May, was one of the swiftest and most complete victories of the Liberator. Three hours were enough to destroy the royalist army and to force its commander to flee to the southwest with some of his men. Many officers were killed, great masses of infantrymen surrendered, 4,000 horses were seized, as well as a great quantity of ammunition, provisions, documents and money.

But the battle of Carabobo was not decisive. Boves was coming to avenge Cagigal. The Liberator distributed his officers with such soldiers as he could gather at different points. Mariño advanced against Boves. Bolívar and Ribas returned to Caracas, still on the endless quest for more resources with which to fight. When complimented upon his victory at Carabobo, Bolívar remarked:

> "Let us not be dazzled by the victories Fate gives us; let us prepare ourselves for greater struggles; let us employ all the resource our good or bad condition, based on the principle that nothing is accomplished when there is something more to do; and we have much still to do."

He was thinking of Boves, Boves who had a large army, all the resources of the plains, and the support of public opinion, while he had neither men nor resources, nor the invigorating approval of his fellow citizens.

Mariño established himself in La Puerta, a place of ill-omen for the patriots, and his position was disadvantageous. When Bolívar arrived to take charge of the army, it was too late to change the place, for Boves was to the front, with three times as many men as there were patriots. It was necessary to fight and it was impossible to conquer. All was lost. A patriot general (Antonio María Freites) killed himself in despair; some officers who had been with Bolívar since the beginning of his glorious career died on the field of battle.

Boves killed all the wounded men and prisoners who fell into his hands. He invited a prisoner colonel (Jalón) to dine with him, and at the end of the meal he ordered him to be hanged and his head sent as a present to his friends at Calabozo.

Mariño escaped in one direction, and Ribas and Bolívar went to Caracas, not without first taking all possible steps to hinder the advance of Boves towards the city. Bolívar was always full of enthusiasm. At that time his most frequent remark was:

> "The art of conquering is learned through defeats."

This battle of La Puerta took place on June 15, 1814. Boves entered the city of La Victoria and then besieged Valencia, which resisted until every means of defense was gone and the defenders were dying of thirst and hunger. Boves proposed capitulation of the besieged and, it being accepted, entered the city on the 10th of July. The treaty provided for the inviolability of the life of all the inhabitants of the city, either military or civilian. Boves had sworn that he would fulfil this convention, but as soon as he had the city in his power he violated his own oath and, with his usual ferocity, put to the sword the governor, the officers, some hundreds of the army, and about ninety of the most prominent inhabitants. His officers forced the young ladies of the families of those who had died to attend a reception in honor of Boves.

Meanwhile, Bolívar was endeavoring to keep enthusiasm alive in Caracas. He even intended to resist the advance of the enemy but, being convinced that the defense of the town would mean a useless sacrifice, he decided to leave it and went east to Barcelona. The inhabitants of

Caracas, realizing the monster Boves was, decided to leave their homes, and a painful pilgrimage ensued. The emigration from Caracas is one of the saddest episodes of the War of Independence. Many emigrants met death on their way east, but they preferred it to the tortures that Boves knew very well how to inflict upon the life and honor of the population of the cities he took. He entered the capital on the 16th of July, and the crimes started. Cagigal, who was a real soldier and a man of honor, saw his authority ignored by Boves. In giving an account of this fact to the government of Spain, the only answer he obtained was that Boves' conduct was approved by Madrid with a vote of thanks for his important services and his great valor.

Leaving his lieutenant, Quero, in command of the city, Boves followed Bolívar. Quero was a native American and was so bad that Boves' rule was preferable to his.

With the few men obtained in Caracas, Bolívar organized a small army with which he protected the emigrants.

From Barcelona he intended to send diplomatic representatives to Europe, thus showing his unshaken confidence in the ultimate triumph of his cause.

With no more than 3,000 men, he faced an army of from 8,000 to 10,000 at Aragua, commanded by Morales, and was defeated (August 18, 1814). A battalion composed of the best elements of the youth of Caracas was entirely destroyed. Bolívar retreated to Barcelona, and Morales entered the town of Aragua, where he massacred more than 3,500 men, women and children, for the sole crime of being Americans. Realizing that he could not hold the city of Barcelona, Bolívar went to the city of Cumaná with generals Ribas and Manuel Piar, the latter famous for his military skill, his daring, his restlessness and his ultimate sad death, of which we shall speak later. From there Bolívar went with Mariño to Carúpano, and then sailed for Cartagena, having lost his reputation and having been insulted by his own officers and friends, among them Piar and Ribas, himself.

Before leaving Venezuela, the Liberator issued a proclamation, for he never neglected an opportunity to speak to his fellow-countrymen and to the world in order to build up favorable public opinion, by which he hoped to win a final victory. In that document Bolívar emphasized the fact that the Spaniards themselves had done very little harm in the fields of battle to the cause of independence, and that defeats were due mainly to the native royalists. This assertion was intended to produce a change of mind on the part of the native population.

> "It seems that Heaven, to grant us at one time humiliation and pride, has permitted that our conquerors be our own brothers, and that our

> brothers only may triumph over us. The army of freedom exterminated the enemy's force, but it could not and should not exterminate the men for whose happiness it fought in hundreds of battles. It is not just to destroy the men who do not want to be free, nor can freedom be enjoyed under strength of arms against the opinion of fanatics whose depraved souls make them love chains as though they were social ties.... Your brothers and not the Spaniards have torn your bosom, shed your blood, set your homes on fire and condemned you to exile."

He then affirmed that he was going to Nueva Granada to render an account of his conduct and to have an impartial judgment, and finished by asserting to the Venezuelans that the people of Nueva Granada would again help them, and that he would always be on the side of liberty.

The East was soon subjected, and all Venezuela was once again under the yoke of Spain, mainly through the work of her own children. During these campaigns Piar and Ribas and the brave General Bermúdez, of whom we shall speak later, were united for a while, but at last each one took his own way. The only good thing that occurred at this time was Boves' death in a battle in December, 1814. Morales was still left as Venezuela's curse.

Ribas, after a defeat, was traveling with two officers. He was sick and sad. He lay down to rest under a tree while his servant went to a near-by town to obtain some provisions. The servant betrayed his master, and Ribas was imprisoned. In the town he was humiliated and insulted. Then he was killed. His head was sent to Caracas and placed in an iron cage at the entrance of the city. His wife, who was Bolívar's aunt, locked herself in a room and swore not to go out until freedom was achieved, and she remained true to her vow.

Bolívar and Mariño arrived in Cartagena on September 25, 1814. The former was on his way to Tunja to render an account of his Venezuelan campaign, when he learned that some Venezuelan troops commanded by General Urdaneta, who were in the territory of Nueva Granada, were quarreling with the native soldiers. He went directly to the army to try to prevent anarchy and dissensions between the Venezuelans and the natives of Nueva Granada. The news proved to be false. The army of Urdaneta, which had left Venezuela to await in the land of Nueva Granada new instructions from the Liberator, and had obtained the protection of that government, received him with the greatest enthusiasm.

From there Bolívar proceeded to Tunja, where he was very well received by Congress. He requested that his conduct be examined and impartially judged. The President of the Congress answered him with the following magnanimous words:

> "General, your country is not vanquished while your sword exists. With this sword you will again rescue her from the power of her oppressors. The Congress of Nueva Granada will give you its protection because it is satisfied with your conduct. You have been an unfortunate general, but you are a great man."

Then the Congress ordered him to liberate Santa Fé (Bogotá), a part of Nueva Granada, which had been separated from the Union. Bolívar with his usual activity proceeded to Bogotá, reached the outskirts of the city and, promising immunity of properties and honor, offered a capitulation. The commander of the garrison refused to accept and an assault followed, the result of which was the surrender of the city. Bolívar was rewarded with the title of *Capitán General* of the Army of the Confederation, and Congress immediately transferred the capital from Tunja to Santa Fé.

Congress asked Bolívar to direct the campaign to protect Nueva Granada against the royalists. So he decided to take Santa Marta, the only place in the country which was still in the hands of the Spaniards; then he planned to fight once more for the liberty of Venezuela. Before adjourning, to meet again in Santa Fé, the Congress at Tunja conferred on Bolívar the official title of Pacificador (Peacemaker), which is frequently used with reference to him, but not so generally as the title he himself used in preference to any other: Libertador.

On this occasion Bolívar could not count on certain troops of Cartagena because of the hostility of Castillo, the commander, who had had differences with Bolívar, and was jealous of his glory. These dissensions hindered Bolívar's advance towards Santa Marta, and produced delays which resulted in great loss of provisions, and also of men because of an epidemic of smallpox which developed in the army. To avoid further dissension, Bolívar was willing to resign without using force against the Cartagena contingent. He was unwilling to permit the royalists to learn of disagreements in the independent army. He had at last, however, to make ready to take the city and was going to lay siege to it when it was learned that a great Spanish army had arrived in Venezuela. The delay of the independent soldiers before Cartagena permitted some royalist troops to take other cities of Nueva Granada, causing great losses of men and arms on different occasions. Bolívar lost 1,000 men; 100 artillery guns and other armament were also lost, as well as the boats upon which the army counted and which would have been very useful to capture the city of Santa Marta. At last, convinced that there was no remedy for the situation, Bolívar determined to resign, and he called for an assembly of his officers, who accepted his resignation. He embarked for Jamaica, first issuing another warning against the disunion of the patriots.

> "No tyrant," he said, "has been destroyed by your arms; they have been stained with the blood of brothers in two struggles which have produced in us an equal sorrow."

The departure of Bolívar was very soon to be deplored by the armies of the independents.

We have mentioned that a Spanish army had arrived in Venezuela, and we must give some details concerning that expedition. Never in the history of the Spanish domination and struggles in America did Spain send such a numerous, well-equipped and powerful army as the one mentioned above. It was commanded by Field-Marshal D. Pablo Morillo.

CHAPTER VIII

1814-1815: BOLÍVAR IN EXILE AND MORILLO IN POWER. THE "JAMAICA LETTER."

At that time Napoleon's luck was beginning to turn in Europe. He had been forced to free Fernando VII, who had been imprisoned since 1808. Fernando VII started to govern his country as a despot, disregarding the national constitution and the public clamor for greater freedom, and soon decided to assert his power in the New World. For that purpose he organized a powerful army, the total strength of which, exclusive of sailors, was nearly ,000 men, supplied with implements for attacks on fortified places, and with everything necessary for warfare on a large scale. This army was placed under the command of Morillo, who also brought with him a number of warships and transports. The soldiers had had experience in the European war and they had proved equal or superior to the armies of Napoleon. The plan was to seize Venezuela and Nueva Granada, then go southward to Perú, and then to Buenos Aires.

Morillo decided to land in the island of Margarita, whose inhabitants had distinguished themselves by their heroism in the long war for independence to such an extent that, upon becoming a province, the island changed its name to New Sparta. Two men of equal bravery, Arismendi and Bermúdez, were in command of a few more than 400 men. Morales was about to lead 5,000 to 6,000 men against the island, with 32 boats, of which 12 were armed with artillery, when Morillo appeared with his huge army. Arismendi decided to surrender. However, Bermúdez would not surrender, and, with reckless daring, he got into a small boat, passed between Morillo's large vessels, insulting the occupants, and then made his escape, going to join the patriots in Cartagena.

Morillo was a very clever soldier; it is said that Wellington himself recommended that he should be chosen, as the Spaniard ablest to subject Venezuela and New Granada. He was as harsh as he was clever, and was ready to wage a war of extermination. By the time Morillo reached the continent, Venezuela was in the hands of Spain. That was at the end of 1814, a fatal year for the cause of independence. From New Spain to the south, the Spanish armies seemed to encounter no resistance. Morillo likened the silence and peace he found everywhere to the silence and peace of the cemeteries. There was no government anywhere, not even military authority. Crime prevailed; cupidity and vengeance were the guiding principles of the chieftains.

After leaving a garrison at Margarita and Cumaná, Morillo went to Caracas, where he arrived on the 11th of May, immediately taking Cagigal's place as captain general. There he published a proclamation announcing that he was ready to go to Nueva Granada with his army, and, after levying exorbitant tributes in money from the citizens and securing in the most outrageous manner all the provisions he could possibly obtain, he sailed from Puerto Cabello for Cartagena with 8,500 men, while Morales with 3,500 advanced by land against the city.

Cartagena resisted the siege in such an admirable manner as to have her name placed side by side with the most heroic cities of history. The besiegers had all kinds of war material; the city lacked all. Still, Cartagena fought constantly during one hundred and six days. The city was then almost in ruins; its inhabitants were starving in the gutters; soldiers and civilians were dying. When Morillo entered its streets he found them almost deserted, and he made the few remaining persons suffer the worst tortures he could devise. The able-bodied men succeeded in escaping by sea.

Several more victories placed all of Nueva Granada in the power of Morillo. The Congress had to dissolve and the Spaniards entered Santa Fé, marking their entrance with the execution of more than 600 Americans, among them men of the greatest prominence and highest social standing. All hope for the liberty of South America seemed to be lost.

Bolívar arrived in Kingston in May, 1815, where he was very well received personally by the governor. But he failed to obtain any substantial help for an expedition to the mainland. Learning of the propaganda being made everywhere against the cause of independence, he once more used his pen to counteract this influence. His most important writing during his stay in Jamaica was a letter addressed on September 6, 1815, to a gentleman of the island, in which he analyzed the causes of the American failure and the reasons he had to hope for the final success of the cause. The "Letter of Jamaica" is counted as one of the greatest documents from the pen of Bolívar.

First, he examines all the errors and crimes committed by the Spaniards in America, describes the partial success of the American armies and the development of the war, as well as the enormous sacrifices made for the cause of independence everywhere, from New Spain to the provinces of the River Plata and Chile. He deprecates the attitude of Europe, which does not intervene to save America from the clutches of an oppressive government, and proves that even for the good of Europe, the independence of America should be secured.

> "Europe itself," he said, "by reasons of wholesome policies, should have prepared and carried out the plan of American independence, not

only because it is so required for the balance of the world, but because this is a legitimate and safe means of obtaining commercial posts on the other side of the ocean."

He very exactly described the true condition of the American people in the following lucid way:

"I consider the actual state of America as when, after the collapse of the Roman Empire, each member constituted a political system in conformity with its interests and position, but with this great difference: that these scattered members reestablished the old nationalities with the alterations required by circumstances or events. But we, who scarcely keep a vestige of things of the past, and who, on the other hand, are not Indians nor Europeans, but a mixture of the legitimate owners of the country and the usurping Spaniards; in short, we, being Americans by birth and with rights equal to those of Europe, have to dispute these rights with the men of the country, and to maintain ourselves against the possession of the invaders. Thus, we find ourselves in the most extraordinary and complicated predicament."

After analyzing slavery in the abstract, he said:

"Americans, under the Spanish system now in vigor, have in society no other place than that of serfs fit for work, and, at the most, that of simple consumers; and even this is limited by absurd restrictions, such as prohibition of the cultivation of European products; the monopoly of certain goods in the hands of the king; the prevention of the establishment in America of factories not possessed by Spain; the exclusive privileges of trade, even regarding the necessities of life; the obstacles placed in the way of the American provinces so that they may not deal with each other, nor have understandings, nor trade. In short, do you want to know what was our lot? The fields, in which to cultivate indigo, cochineal, coffee, sugar cane, cocoa, cotton; the solitary plains, to breed cattle; the deserts, to hunt the wild beasts; the bosom of the earth, to extract gold, with which that avaricious country was never satisfied."

* * * *

"We were never viceroys or governors except by very extraordinary reasons; archbishops and bishops, seldom; ambassadors, never; military men, only as subordinates; nobles, without privileges; lastly, we were neither magistrates nor financiers, and hardly merchants. All this we had to accept in direct opposition to our institutions.

"The Americans have risen suddenly and without previous preparation and without previous knowledge and, what is more deplorable, without experience in public affairs, to assume in the world the eminent dignity of legislators, magistrates, administrators of the public treasury, diplomats, generals and all the supreme and subordinate authorities which form the hierarchy of an organized state.

"The events of the mainland have proved that perfectly representative institutions do not agree with our character, habits, and present state of enlightenment.... So long as our fellow citizens do not acquire the talents and the political virtues which distinguish our brothers of the North, who have a system of government altogether popular in character, I am very much afraid these institutions might lead to our ruin instead of aiding us....

"I desire more than anybody else to see the formation in America the greatest nation in the world, not so much as to its extension and wealth as to its glory and freedom."

* * * *

"Monsignor de Pradt has wisely divided America into fifteen or seventeen independent states, ruled by as many monarchs. I agree on the first point, for America could be divided into seventeen countries As for the second point, although it is easier to realize, it is less useful, and, consequently, I am not in favor of American monarchies. Here are my reasons: The real interests of a republic are circumscribed in the sphere of its conservation, prosperity and glory. Since freedom is not imperialistic, because it is opposed to empires, no impulse induces Repúblicans to extend the limits of their country; injuring its own center, with only the object of giving their neighbors a liberal constitution. They do not acquire any right nor any advantage by conquering them, unless they reduce them to colonies, conquered territories or allies, following the example of Rome.... A state too large in itself, or together with its dependent territories, finally decays and its free form reverts to a tyrannical one, the principles which should conserve it relax, and at last it evolves into despotism. The characteristic of the small republics is permanency; that of the large ones is varied, but always tends to an empire. Almost all of the former have been of long duration; among the latter Rome alone lived for some centuries, but this was because the capital was a republic, and the rest of her dominions were not, for they governed themselves by different laws and constitutions."

Then Bolívar ventures to prophesy the destiny of all nations of the continent, from Mexico to the River Plata, and he does so with such accuracy of vision that almost to the word the history of the first half century of independence in Latin America was shaped according to his prediction. The tranquility of Chile, the tyranny of Rosas in Argentina, the Mexican empire, all were clearly seen in the future by his genius. Near the close of his letter, he adds these inspired words:

> "How beautiful it would be if the Isthmus of Panamá should come to be to us what the Isthmus of Corinth was to the Greeks! May God g that some day we may have the happiness of installing there an august congress of the representatives of the republics, kingdoms and empires, to discuss and study the high interests of peace and war with the nations of the other three parts of the world! This kind of cooperation may be established in some happy period of our regeneration...."

He ends this capital document of his career as a political writer, by pleading again for union as the only means of putting an end to Spanish domination, in America.

Nothing better can be said than the following words of a biographer of Bolívar:[6]

> "Alone, poor, in a foreign land, when his friends had denied him and had persecuted him, and his enemies had torn him to shreds in blind rage, when everybody saw America carrying once again the yoke imposed upon her, Bolívar saw her redeemed, and from the depth of his soul he felt himself bound to this wonderful task of redemption. His spirit, animated by an unknown breath, and which had lived a superior life, saw Colombia free, Chile established, Argentina expanding, Mexico and Perú liberated, the Isthmus of Panamá converted into the center of communications and activities of human industry; it saw South America divided into powerful nationalities, having passed from slavery to struggle and to the conquest of her own dignity, and from the times of the sword to those of political civilization and organization of power; national units weighty in the statistics of the world by reason of their products, by their commerce, by their culture, by their wars, their alliances, their laws, their free governments; with names of their own, with famous histories, with supreme virtues. All that Bolívar saw, and of all that Bolívar wrote. Can human intelligence go any farther?"

6 Larrazábal, "Vida del Libertador Simón Bolívar," Vol. I. page 404.

CHAPTER IX

1815-1817: BOLÍVAR'S EXPEDITION AND NEW EXILE. HE GOES TO GUAYANA.

While in Jamaica, Bolívar was as active as he had been in Venezuela. While he used his pen to teach the world the meaning of the South American Revolution, and to try and obtain friends for the cause of freedom, he worked actively in the Island and in other parts of the West Indies to organize an expedition to the continent.

In this work he was very greatly helped by Luis Brion,—a wealthy merchant of Curaçao,—who sacrificed practically all of his private fortune in helping the cause of Liberty.

The influence exercised by the Holy Alliance on the governments of Europe had some effect on the authorities of Jamaica, who hindered the assembling of munitions of war by Bolívar. He then decided to go to the Republic of Haiti, after having escaped almost by a miracle, an assassin who, believing that he was asleep in a hammock where he usually rested, stabbed to death a man occupying Bolívar's customary place. The assassin was a slave set free by Bolívar.

On his way to Haiti he learned of the surrender of Cartagena. The President of Haiti, Alexander Pétion, received Bolívar in a most friendly way, and gave him very substantial assistance in the preparations for his expedition to the continent. The men who had succeeded in escaping from Cartagena were also well received by Pétion, and treated in a most hospitable manner. Among them many were personal enemies of Bolívar. None the less, Bolívar was elected supreme head of the expedition, and the refugees from Cartagena followed him in his new undertaking, with Mariño as Major General of the Army and Brion as Admiral. About 250 persons constituted the party, but they carried enough ammunition to arm six thousand men, whom they hoped to gather together on the continent. Once more Bolívar seemed to undertake the impossible, but, as ever, he had full confidence in the ultimate triumph of liberty. The proportion of his enemies to his followers was 100 to 1. Public opinion was still against him, but he was still the same man who, at that time more than any other, had become a symbol—the symbol of America's freedom.

Bolívar made his way to the Island of Margarita, where the Spanish commander had systematically carried on a work of destruction of wealth and humiliation of families.

In November of 1815, Arismendi, the man who had submitted to Morillo, again proclaimed independence in the Island and started to fight with no better arms than clubs and farm implements. The Governor determined to destroy the population of the Island, even allowing his anger to fall on Arismendi's own wife,—but Arismendi continued fighting and, knowing his attitude, Bolívar decided to come to Margarita before touching the continent. On that island Bolívar reorganized the government of the Republic in its third period and was again proclaimed Supreme Chief of the Republic, while Mariño was designated Second Chief. Then Bolívar called for the election of deputies and proclaimed that he would stop the War to Death, provided the Spaniards would also stop waging war in a ruthless way. The Captain General answered by offering 10,000 pesos for the head of either Bolívar, Bermúdez, Mariño, Piar, Brion or Arismendi. From Margarita the undaunted Libertador went to the continent, landing in Carúpano, from which place he sent Mariño to fight in the east, in the land of his old victories, where he was well known; and organized a military school to prepare officers, and worked with his usual activity in the organization of the army, while a popular assembly gathered in the city and again accepted Bolívar as Supreme Chief. Mariño and Piar, the latter fostering the ambitions of the former, started again to act against the orders of the Libertador. Several partial defeats made the condition of the insurgents so critical that Bolívar made up his mind to leave the east and commence operations in the west, as he had previously done. On July 6, he and his men landed in Ocumare de la Costa, a port north of Valencia, proclaimed the cessation of the War to Death, and offered pardon to all those who surrendered, even though they were Spaniards. He also proclaimed the freedom of all slaves, thereby fulfilling a promise made to President Pétion of Haiti.

> "Henceforward," he said, "in Venezuela, there will be only one class of men: all will be citizens."

From there Brion was sent to do as much damage as possible to the Spanish sea trade, and he also received a commission to get in touch with the government of Washington, and with the patriots of Mexico. The royalists organized a strong veteran army and attacked Bolívar, who, with his inexperienced soldiers, could not resist, and had to leave Ocumare. One of his followers, called MacGregor, who had been sent with some men by Bolívar into the interior of the country, decided to go and join the guerrillas who were fighting the royalists in the interior; and his daring movement was crowned with success, for he and his men advanced through the plains, fighting the royalists, or dodging them when they were too numerous to be fought. In that way they covered a distance of over four hundred miles, at last joining the forces fighting near the Orinoco. Again deprived of his prestige, Bolívar was deposed and Mariño and Bermúdez were elected first and second chiefs. Bolívar had to return to Haiti. His deposition was not well received by the chiefs of the guerrillas, who were fighting the royalists in the interior. Bolívar—undaunted as ever—thought only of organizing an expedition to assist those who were fighting in Venezuela. Pétion once more rendered him substantial aid. He was invited to go to Mexico and help in the War of Independence of New Spain, but he declined, and instead continued to make preparations to go back to fight for his country.

The different commanders had obtained some partial successes, but they soon recognized the necessity of Bolívar's leadership, and sent Arismendi to Port-au-Prince to ask him to return. Admiral Brion also besought him to go back to Venezuela. At the end of December Bolívar reached Margarita Island with some Venezuelan exiles. Once there, he issued a proclamation convoking an assembly, for his paramount desire was to have the military power subordinated to the civil government.

On January 1, 1817, Bolívar once more set foot on the continent, this time never to leave it. The lessons learned through failures had been well learned, and new plans were taking shape in his mind. He was thinking of the freedom of all America, not only of Venezuela, and started plans for the freedom of New Granada and Perú: all this when he had no soldiers to command, except 400 men under Arismendi, to which 300 were added by conscription. He advanced towards Caracas, but was defeated, and had to return to Barcelona, leaving all his war provisions in the hands of the enemy. He then had 600 men, and he knew that an army of over 5,000 royalists was advancing against the city. At first he thought of resisting the enemy, counting on the help of Mariño, who was at that time in the South, and who, in fact, hastened to the rescue. Mariño and Bermúdez entered Barcelona and Bolívar received them with joy. Nevertheless, he understood that he could not stay in that city. It was clear that the best method of resistance would consist in attacking the royalists from different and unexpected angles. He concluded that he must leave Barcelona and go to the Orinoco Valley and the Province of Guayana (Venezuelan Guiana). Several of his officers opposed the idea so strongly that at last Bolívar was induced to leave some men to protect the city and send the rest to Guayana, under the command of Mariño. The men left in Barcelona were sacrificed by the royalists. In April Bolívar crossed the Orinoco and afterwards met Piar, who was besieging the City of Angostura, the most important position of Guayana. Piar had been fighting in that section with some success since the end of 1816.

The inconstancy of Mariño showed itself once more, although in this instance his conduct was opposed by Bermúdez and other officers. He did not give opportune help to Barcelona, and tried to foster his own ambitions instead of collaborating with Bolívar. Without the support of Mariño and with Barcelona lost, Bolívar found himself in a very difficult situation, counting more on his own genius than on human help. Morillo, master of Nueva Granada, had come from Santa Fé and destroyed most of the insurgent forces existing in the western part of Venezuela. He had received more reinforcements from Spain. Bolívar, nevertheless, continued his work with his all powerful faith, trying to have his dreams proved true by the effort of his will. "We shall conquer them and we shall free America," he used to say. The greatest support that Bolívar found at that time was that of General Piar's troops.

In order to supplant Bolívar, Mariño convoked a congress, which proved to be a farce, having but ten members. Mariño solemnly resigned his place of second in command of the army and also resigned on behalf of Bolívar, without the slightest authorization from his chief. The "congress" appointed Mariño supreme chief of the army and decided to establish the capital of the republic in Margarita. The other heads of the army refused to recognize the usurper, and many of them, among whom the foremost was Colonel Antonio José Sucre, went to Guayana to join the legitimate commander. Mariño himself at last abruptly dissolved the congress. Bolívar, with his usual prudence, did not show that he noticed the attitude of his second, and praised General Piar for his triumphs, knowing, nevertheless, by that time, that he could not count on the personal loyalty of the latter.

While attending to the operations of the siege Bolívar did not neglect his usual administrative work. He organized a system of military justice so as to avoid the arbitrariness of the military chieftains and, being aware that Piar had tried to foster the disloyalty of Mariño, he endeavored to convince him of his folly, and said very plainly that unless these machinations were stopped, great evils must be expected.

Admiral Brion came with his boats to the Orinoco in order to help in the siege of Angostura. When he arrived in the river, the royalists of Angostura decided to abandon the city, which fell into the hands of the independents, Bermúdez being the first to occupy it. Bolívar found himself for the first time behind his enemy and was ready to fight against his foes in the position that his foes had held in the past. He obtained, besides, great resources in cattle and horses, and it seemed possible that he might obtain the coöperation of the plainsmen of the Apure Valley, the old followers of Boves, now followers of José Antonio Páez, a lover of personal liberty and a sworn foe of the Spanish régime.

CHAPTER X

1817-1818: PIAR'S DEATH. VICTORY OF CALABOZO. SECOND DEFEAT AT LA PUERTA. SUBMISSION OF PÁEZ.

Morillo, who had lost a great part of his army and his prestige trying to conquer the Island of Margarita, was obliged to withdraw when he discovered that Bolívar had become master of Guayana. The two leaders were soon again confronting each other on the mainland.

Bolívar, who had always been conciliatory towards his personal enemies and who had tried to make friends with all the chieftains, had been constantly preaching union among all the elements fighting for independence. He had, however, met with slight success, and a moment came when he realized that he must use strong measures in order to have discipline in his army. Piar tried to induce certain officers to establish a council for the purpose of curtailing the authority of Bolívar. The Liberator tried persuasion, but failed. Piar decided to leave the army. He pretended to be sick and, offering to go to one of the islands of the Caribbean, requested leave of absence, which was granted.

Once having obtained his leave of absence, he became Bolívar's open foe; he remained in Venezuela and came back to Angostura, where he intrigued with other chieftains, and tried to get the support of Bermúdez to deprive Bolívar of his command. Peaceful means failing again to win over Piar, Bolívar ordered his apprehension. Piar fled to Mariño, and began enlisting soldiers to resist. He enjoyed great prestige; he had been a distinguished general and in bravery, daring, skill and personal magnetism, no one surpassed him. Bolívar referred with his officers and, after being assured of the support of all, he ordered the apprehension of Piar, who was abandoned by his own followers and fell into the hands of Bolívar's agents.

Piar was court-martialed and was sentenced to death. Bolívar confirmed the sentence and Piar died with the same bravery and serenity he had shown on the field of battle. Bolívar deplored the fate of the valiant general, but with this action succeeded in obtaining a greater measure of respect and obedience from the army than he had been able to secure with his former leniency.

As a measure of justice and wisdom, Bolívar, on the 3rd of September, 1817, decreed the distribution of national wealth among the officers and soldiers of the Republic as a reward for their services. A council of state was established, and the General rendered to it an account of his work and presented an exposition of the state of the national affairs.

In his address he explained the division of the powers of the state, and freely praised all the generals of the insurgent army, mentioning General Páez, the chieftain of the *llaneros* (plainsmen), who was the terror of the royalists and whose support was becoming of paramount importance to the Liberator. He declared that Angostura was to be the provisional capital of Venezuela until the city of Caracas could be retaken from the royalists. Then he divided the administration into three sections,—state and finance, war and navy, and interior and justice, putting in each the man best prepared for the position.

In order to carry out his decision to advance against Caracas, he first made sure that he could count on the assistance of Páez. The latter agreed to fight in combination with Bolívar on condition that he would be absolutely independent and have full power in the territory under his command. Páez was one of the most remarkable characters of the revolution of independence and the early years of Venezuela. He was a young man when he came in touch with Bolívar,—strong, attractive, every inch a warrior, who lived with his plainsmen just as they lived, living with, and caring for, his horse as the others did, eating the same food as they did, and fighting whenever a chance presented itself. He was ignorant. He was opposed to discipline and his men knew none,—they followed him because of his prestige and because he was one of them, but better than any of them. His men were the same kind Boves had commanded, and as Boves was terrible with his horsemen, so was Páez, with the exception that Páez fought for the cause of liberty and did not stain his life with the monstrosities of the Spanish chieftain. His name was respected in the southwestern part of Venezuela, and he was ready to fight against the army of Morillo when he received the message of Bolívar.

Morillo concentrated his army in Calabozo, the center of the plains, intending to attack Páez in Apure, and other patriots who operated to the south under Zaraza. Bolívar sent General Pedro León Torres to support the latter, but they were defeated in the bloody battle of La Hogaza.

Bolívar began his movement to join Páez, full of confidence in spite of the check at La Hogaza. It was now 1818. He was wont to say "This year will see the end of the Spanish power in Venezuela." His faith had more foundation than during his exile and the earlier expeditions, when, with a handful of men, he had started to fight against the great armies organized by the Spanish government. Public opinion was now beginning to swing towards him; he had Páez and his plainsmen on his side and he counted on the great resources of Guayana.

His activity was astonishing. In a month and a half, he and his men traveled 900 miles to join Páez. As they advanced, his forces were being disciplined, organized, strengthened and made ready to fight. Owing to his personal prestige, and his unbelievable daring, Páez was of inestimable value. On one occasion he promised Bolívar to have boats at a certain place so that the army could cross the Apure River. When Bolívar arrived at the point in question with the army, he found that there were no boats ready. When Páez was questioned by the Libertador, he replied:

"Oh, yes, Sir, I am counting on the boats."

"But where are they?" Bolívar asked.

"The enemy has them," said Páez, indicating some royalists' launches and canoes across the river.

While Bolívar was wondering what Páez meant by that, the latter called fifty of his men and with them jumped into the river with their unsaddled horses, swam through it, defeated the enemy, and brought the boats across. Bolívar's forces were then able to pass. Immediately the armies of independence advanced to Calabozo, with such swiftness that Morillo knew of their advance only when they had arrived. The Spaniards were utterly defeated and Morillo himself barely escaped falling prisoner. Bolívar could have advanced and finished the destruction of the royalist army, but Páez and other officers were opposed to this course, and the commander-in-chief had to yield.

Soon after this, Bolívar was again in La Victoria, between Valencia and Caracas, having occupied the rich valley of Aragua, in which he had lived as a young man of wealth, and had passed years of suffering. He immediately sent proclamations ordering all men able to fight to present themselves with arms and horses for the service of the Republic. He called on those who had been slaves to defend their own freedom, and urged the manufacture and repair of arms. His position was by no means secure. Morillo was in Valencia, and don Miguel de Latorre, the victor of La Hogaza, was in Caracas. A triumph of Morillo over some patriots near Valencia forced the Liberator to retreat in haste from La Victoria. When Morillo learned of his retreat, he immediately went on with his persecution and at last met the independent army in a place called La Puerta, where, on March 15, 1818, he inflicted on Bolívar perhaps the greatest of his defeats, although at great loss to himself, and suffering severe wounds. The Spanish authorities thought that Bolívar would never recover from this disaster, but soon the undaunted Liberator was again fighting the royal forces.

The defeat of La Puerta was so costly to the royalists that they did not dare to occupy the position. It was considered so important, however, for the cause of Spain that Morillo was rewarded with the title of Marquis of La Puerta. Morillo waited for reinforcements to be sent to him by the Spanish commander of Caracas, Latorre; and Bolívar, who never despaired, immediately got ready for new struggles. He summoned Páez to his aid and prepared for the defense of Calabozo, so that when Latorre arrived he found a well organized army under command of the Liberator. He withdrew, and Bolívar followed him, fighting an indecisive battle.

Convinced that he could not at that time occupy Caracas, Bolívar decided to consolidate his position in the West, and sent his troops towards the city of San Carlos, while he worked actively in Calabozo, and elsewhere through his lieutenants, to increase his army. Then he went to join Páez, was surprised and defeated on his way, being in imminent danger himself. Furthermore, through a partial defeat of Páez and disasters of other officers, by the end of May the insurgent forces were almost totally destroyed. Morales, of bloody reputation, had taken Calabozo; and, in the East, fate was against the independents, where the weakness of Mariño had caused the loss of Cumaná. In other sections, the troops had rebelled against the authority of Bolívar, and had begun to fight in the same desultory way as before. All this was not sufficient to shake the constancy and faith of Bolívar. He addressed a letter to Pueyrredón, Supreme Director of the Provinces of the River Plata, using these lofty words:

> "Venezuela is now in mourning, but tomorrow, covered with laurels, she will have extinguished the last of the tyrants who now desecrate her soil. Then she will invite you to a single association, so that our motto may be 'Unity in South America.' All Americans should have one country."

Back in Angostura, with his unflinching courage, he went on reviving his army and reorganizing the supreme government, which had been in the hands of the Council of State during his absence. He appointed secretaries of the cabinet and established a weekly paper to spread the new principles of the government. He again entrusted Mariño with the command of the province of Cumaná, took the necessary steps to suppress the symptoms of indiscipline in the army, and initiated several military operations. Again, when his means were more limited, his thoughts covered a greater field. He seemed unable to assure the liberty of Venezuela, yet he was thinking of giving freedom to Nueva Granada. He sent a proclamation to its inhabitants and directed one of his generals to invade it. He said:

> "The day of America has arrived, and no human power can stop the course of nature, guided by the hand of Providence. Join your efforts to those of your brethren. Venezuela goes with me to free you, as you in the past with me gave freedom to Venezuela.... The sun will not end the course of its present period without seeing altars dedicated to liberty throughout your territory."

This promise came true.

Before undertaking this great task, he convoked a national assembly for January 1, 1819. In his long proclamation summoning the representatives of the people he again made a summary of the work already done, and asked the people to select the best citizens for the places, without regard to the fact that they might or might not have been in the army of freedom.

> "For my part," he stated, "I renounce forever the authority you have conferred upon me, and, while the fearful Venezuelan war lasts, I shall accept none save that of a simple soldier. The first day of peace will be the last of my command."

Venezuela had lost the best of her blood; she was nothing better than a heap of ruins, and yet, she was preparing for new and greater undertakings.

After publishing the proclamation, he started for Cumaná. Learning that Mariño had been defeated, he sent him to Barcelona, and returned to Angostura to organize new armies. Spain, he knew, was trying to obtain the help of the other nations of Europe to regain possession of her American colonies. He felt it expedient, therefore, once more to manifest to the world the attitude of Venezuela regarding her new relations with the mother country. He published a decree on November 20, 1818, reaffirming the principles of independence proclaimed on July 5, 1811. This decree was published and translated into three languages, to be distributed all over the world. After stating the reasons for its publication, he emphatically declared that Venezuela was free and did not contemplate further dealings with Spain, nor was she willing ever to deal with Spain except as her equal, in peace and in war, as is done reciprocally by all countries. He concluded with the following words, which represent clearly his character and that of his followers:

> "The Republic of Venezuela declares that from April 19, 1810, she has been fighting for her rights; that she has shed most of her sons' blood, that she has sacrificed her youth, all her pleasures, and all that is dear and sacred to men, in order to regain her sovereign rights and in order to keep them in their integrity, as Divine Providence granted them to her; the Venezuelan people have decided to bury themselves in the ruins of their country if Spain, Europe and the world insist on subjecting them to the Spanish yoke."

Immediately afterwards, Bolívar had to go to the West, where Páez had been proclaimed supreme director of the republic by some dissenters. Bolívar talked with Páez in private, induced him to return to obedience and submission, and promoted him to major general in command of the independent cavalry. The Liberator then returned to install the national congress and to make preparations for the liberation of Nueva Granada.

CHAPTER XI

1819: THE CONGRESS OF ANGOSTURA. A GREAT ADDRESS. CAMPAIGNING IN THE PLAINS.

Congress did not meet until February 15, 1819, on account of the late arrival of some representatives. There again Bolívar spoke, and on this occasion he excelled himself in expressing his ideas regarding freedom.[7]

> "Happy is the citizen," he said in his address, "who, under the shield of the armies he commands, has convoked national sovereignty to exercise its absolute will.... Only a forceful need, coupled with the imperious will of the people, could force me into the terrible and hazardous position of Dictator and Supreme Chief of the Republic. I breathe freely now when I return to you this authority, which, with much danger, difficulty and sorrow, I have succeeded in keeping in the midst of the most horrible misfortunes which can befall a people."

Among the most remarkable parts of this document, the following will bear close and careful study:

> "The continuation of authority in one individual has frequently been the undoing of democratic governments. Repeated elections are essential in popular systems, because nothing is so dangerous as to permit a citizen to remain long in power. The people get used to obeying and he gets used to commanding it, from which spring usurpation and tyranny." ... "We have been subjected by deception rather than by force. We have been degraded by vice rather than by superstition. Slavery is a child of darkness; an ignorant people becomes a blind instrument of its own destruction. It takes license for freedom, treachery for patriotism, vengeance for justice." ... "Liberty is a rich food, but of difficult digestion. Our weak fellow citizens must greatly strengthen their spirit before

7 Bolívar has been accused of verbosity. Of all the accusations, this is one of the most stupid. Bolívar's style is the style of his epoch. The Spanish and French writers of that period wrote exactly in the same form, and if his words do not appear as modern and sober as we might wish them at this time, we must remember that times alter customs, and styles also, and that if a document of Bolívar's were judged with no knowledge of the work realized by the great man of the South, it might appear bombastic; when his life is known, his words seem altogether natural. He was proud, and his words show it, but his pride was a collective pride rather than an individual one. He praised the work of the liberators, while he was the Liberator *par excellence*, with this title conferred upon him officially. When he mentioned his own person and his own glory, he did not exceed the language of men of his time, and employed words even inferior to his own merits. He was as emphatic as his race is, but he was never pedantic, and as for the vanity of which Lorain Petre accuses him and his race, it never existed. Lorain Petre's pamphlet is a work of passion masquerading as one of wisdom and of impartiality.

they are able to digest the wholesome and nutritious bread of liberty." ... "The most perfect system of government is the one which produces the greatest possible happiness, the greatest degree of social safety, and the greatest political stability."

The following study of the balance of powers in a country shows keen political penetration:

> "In republics, the executive must be the stronger, because all conspire against him; while in monarchies, the legislative power should be the stronger, because all conspire in favor of the monarch. The splendor of the throne, of the crown, of the purple; the formidable support given to it by the nobility; the immense wealth which generations accumulate in the same dynasty; the fraternal protection which kings mutually enjoy, are considerable advantages which militate in favor of royal authority and make it almost boundless. These advantages show the need of giving a Repúblican executive a greater degree of authority than that possessed by a constitutional prince.
>
> "A Repúblican executive is an individual isolated in the midst of society, to restrain the impulses of the people toward license and the propensities of administrators to arbitrariness. He is directly subject to the legislative power, to the people; he is a single man, resisting the combined attack of opinion, personal interests and the passions of society."

Elsewhere in his address, he remarks:

> "The government of Venezuela has been, is, and must be Repúblican its foundation must be the sovereignty of the people, the division of powers, civil freedom, the proscription of slavery, the abolition of monarchy and of privileges." ... "Unlimited freedom, absolute democracy, are the rocks upon which Repúblican hopes have been destroyed. Look at the old republics, the modern republics, and the republics now in process of formation; almost all have aimed to establish themselves as absolutely democratic, and almost all have failed in their just desires." ... "Angels only, and not men, could exist free, peaceful and happy, while all of them exercise sovereign power." ... "Let the legislative power relinquish the attributes belonging to the executive, but let it acquire, nevertheless, new influence in the true balance of authority. Let the courts be strengthened by the stability and independence of the judges the establishment of juries, and of civil and criminal codes, not prescribed by old times, nor by conquering kings, but by the voice of nature, by the clamor of justice and by the genius of wisdom." ... "Humankind cries against the thoughtless and blind legislators who have thought that they might with impunity try chimerical institutions. All the peoples of the world have attempted to gain freedom, some by deeds of arms, others by laws passing alternately from anarchy to despotism, from despotism to anarchy. Very few have contented themselves with moderate ambitions constituting themselves

in conformity with their means, their spirit and their circumstances. Let us not aspire to impossible things, lest, desiring to rise above the region of freedom, we descend to the region of tyranny. From absolute liberty, peoples invariably descend to absolute power, and the means between those two extremes is social liberty." ... "In order to constitute a stable government, a national spirit is required as a foundation, having for its object a uniform aspiration toward two capital principles; moderation of popular will and limitation of public authority." ... "Popular education must be the first care of the paternal love of Congress. Morals and enlightenment are the two poles of a republic; morals and enlightenment are our first needs."

Then Bolívar recommended the sanctioning of his decree granting freedom to the slaves.

"I abandon to your sovereign decision the reform or abrogation of all my statutes and decrees, but I implore for the confirmation of the absolute freedom of slaves as I would implore for my own life and the life of the Republic."

This document might well be quoted in its entirety. Very few in the history of mankind can compare with it. "No one has ever spoken like this man," says an author.[8] The peoples of America have been marching steadily, though at times haltingly, but always in a progressive way, towards the ideals of Bolívar. The Congress of Angostura carried into effect many of these sublime principles.

"An assembly of tried and illustrious men, the Congress of Angostura, responded to the important requirements of the revolution, and when it gave birth to Colombia, powerful and splendid, it realized no longer a task Venezuelan in character, but rather an American mission."[9]

"The address of the Liberator in Angostura may be considered as a masterpiece of reason and patriotism."[10]

At the beginning the Congress was formed of twenty-six deputies, which number was increased to twenty-nine, representing the provinces of Caracas, Barcelona, Cumaná, Barinas, Guayana, Margarita and Casanare. This last province belonged to Nueva Granada and the others forming the same vice-royalty were expected to be represented as soon as freed from Spanish domination. Its president was don Francisco Antonio Zea.

As was proper Bolívar immediately divested himself of the civil authority, handing it to the President of the Congress and then resigned his

8 Larrazábal—*Vida de Simón Bolívar*. Vol. 2, p. 177.
9 *Discurso de Bolívar en el Congreso de Angostura,*—Caracas.—1919.
10 Larrazábal—*Vida de Simón Bolívar*. Vol. 2, p. 177.

command of the army, offering to serve in any military position, in which he pledged himself to give an example of subordination and of the "blind obedience which should distinguish every soldier of the Republic." The Congress, as was to be expected, confirmed Bolívar in his command and sanctioned all the commissions he had given during the campaign. He was also elected President of the Republic, with don Francisco Antonio Zea as Vice-President to take charge of the government during the campaigns of the Liberator. He organized the government, made the appointments for the cabinet and sent commissioners to England to obtain arms, ammunition and a loan of a million pounds sterling, undertakings in which the Republic did not meet with success at that time.

The installation of the Congress made a great impression at home and abroad, in spite of the attacks and ridicule with which the Spaniards tried to discredit it. On that eventful day Bolívar saw his dream of a great nation, Colombia, take shape, even though it were in danger of dying shortly after its birth.

After asking all the members of the government and prominent persons of Angostura to remain united in the cause of liberty, he went to join the army in the western section.

During his stay in Angostura and afterwards he had been receiving foreign contingents, especially from England. The Foreign Legion played from that time on a very important role in the War of Independence and helped substantially to obtain the triumph. By means of the British contingents, the plainsmen of Páez, the regular armies of Bermúdez and Mariño, and the genius of Bolívar, which united and directed all, the final victory was achieved.

After a rapid march, Bolívar joined Páez and for a while waged a constant war in the plains, consisting of local actions by which he slowly, but surely, destroyed the morale of the royalists and did all the harm he could, the climate being a great factor in his favor. He was impetuous by nature, but for a while he imitated Fabius by slowly gnawing at the strength of his foe. He tired him with marches and surprises. He burned the grass of the plains, cleared away the cattle, and drove Morillo to the point of desperation. Meanwhile he lived the same life as the *llaneros*, for he could do whatever the semi-barbarous plainsmen did. He could ride on the bare back of a horse against the foe, or just for the exhilaration of crossing the endless plains with the swiftness of lightning; he could groom his horse and he did; he swam the rivers, waded marshes, slept on the ground and associated freely with his men in the moonlight in front of the camp fires.

At this point of the war, Páez again distinguished himself by an act of supreme daring. With 150 of his horsemen, he crossed the river

Arauca, which separated the independent army from the royalists, and then feigned a retreat along the river, which in very few places could be waded. Morillo, considering him and his men easy prey, sent 1,200 men, including all his cavalry, against the retreating horsemen. When they were far from the main body of the army Páez rushed against the attacking party, without giving them time to organize, and at the first inrush he destroyed the column. The defeated royalists fled to their camp and Morillo decided to withdraw, which he did during the night. This action, fought on April 3, 1819, and known as the Battle of Las Queseras del Medio, covered Páez with glory and Morillo with discredit. Bolívar conferred all the honors and praise possible on the brave Páez and on his men.

At that time the plains began to be flooded. In the northern part of South America, the season of rain, called winter, lasts from May until October. The Valley of the Orinoco becomes in places an interior sea. The cattle go up to the highlands and, where horses walk in the summer, small boats ply in the winter, going from village to village and from home to home. The villages are built on piles, and traveling on horseback is very difficult during this season. On these plains, Bolívar and his men would travel, riding or swimming as required. They would drive cattle with them and kill them for food, pressing the remaining meat under the saddles, and continuing the march. To all of this the plainsmen were accustomed; and to this, Bolívar, born among the greatest comforts and reared amid all the refinements of life, showed no apparent repugnance.

CHAPTER XII

1819: BOLÍVAR PAYS HIS DEBT TO NUEVA GRANADA. BOYACÁ, A DREAM COMES TRUE.

Páez was commissioned to get fresh horses with which to advance against Barinas, when Bolívar got in communication with the province of Nueva Granada—where Santander, a very able general, had organized an army, which was fighting successfully against the royalists. Bolívar perhaps recalled his promise made to Nueva Granada before leaving Angostura, or perhaps he obeyed a long prepared plan. The fact is that he decided to do nothing less than cross the flooded plains, go to the viceroyalty, free that country from the Spanish domination and return to emancipate Venezuela. The man who could not consider himself even the equal of Morillo again dreamed of the impossible, and decided to convert it into fact.

He convoked his officers, communicated to them his plan of leaving some men to distract Morillo's attention while he, himself, should go quickly to Nueva Granada and give it freedom, and on May 25, 1819, he started to carry out his project, one perhaps more difficult than those of Hannibal and Napoleon.

He left Páez to hold the attention of the royalists, and, besides that depletion, had to suffer the loss of many of his plainsmen who refused to accompany him across the Andes. But Colonel Rook, the head of the British Legion, assured Bolívar that he would follow him "beyond Cape Horn, if necessary." After spending a month painfully wading through the flooded plains, he ascended the Andes and crossed them, in spite of inexpressible suffering. The men had lost most of their clothing in the marshes below; very few soldiers had even a pair of trousers in good condition. Leaving the torrid climate of the plains, these men had to climb up the Andes almost naked, on foot,—because they could not use their horses,—and to suffer the freezing cold of the summits. Many died, but the faith of Bolívar sustained the rest. The Liberator himself suffered all the fatigue of the road. He was worn out, but he was always going forward.

Then he began his fight with the royalists in the land of Nueva Granada. At this time he had no horses and his men had had to abandon most of the provisions and ammunition. While in these straits, he learned that a royalist army of 5,000 well disciplined men was approaching. Bolívar had three days only in which to get ready, but at the end of that short period he had arms and horses provided and his men prepared to fight. Then he attacked the enemy, at first by the system of guerrillas and later in formal battle, in which his genius succeeded in defeating the disciplined strength of his foes. On entering the emancipated cities he was received with the greatest enthusiasm and acclaimed as their liberator. New recruits joined him everywhere.

These pitched battles would receive greater mention in history were it not for the fact that another one took place almost immediately afterwards which, by its magnitude and its results, made the others sink to a secondary place. The royalists took position in a place called Boyacá. They were commanded by Barreiro, and formed the vanguard of the army of the viceroy Sámano. Bolívar attacked them with an army only two-thirds their size and was victorious. Among the independents was José Antonio Anzoátegui, a major general, who fought like a hero and succeeded in breaking the stubborn resistance of the enemy. Death spared him on the field of battle, but his glorious career ended a few days after the victory of Boyacá, following a short illness. He was thirty years old. A member of a very distinguished family, his culture was brilliant, his character was pure, his loyalty and patriotism were unsurpassed. His loss was equivalent to a great defeat. Barreiro, the commander of the royalists, fell prisoner to Bolívar's troops. This battle occurred on August 7, 1819, and was not only a complete victory for the forces of independence, but also meant practically the end of the Spanish régime in Nueva Granada.

Regarding the crossing of the Andes and the victory of Boyacá, J.E. Rodó (Uruguayan), one of the greatest thinkers of recent years, says:

> "Other crossings of mountains may have been more adroit and more exemplary strategy; none so audacious, so heroic and legendary. Twenty-five hundred men climb the eastern slope of the range, and a smaller number of specters descends the other side; these specters are those of the men who were strong in body and soul, for the weak ones remained in the snow, in the torrents, on the heights where the air is not sufficient for human breasts. And with those specters of survivors, the victory of Boyacá was obtained."[11]

One of the elements required for the upbuilding of Colombia—the independence of Nueva Granada, was created by the victory of Boyacá. This was by its effects the greatest triumph of Bolívar up to that moment. The Liberator advanced to Bogotá and was received there in a frenzy of admiration and love.

The whole march and campaign lasted 75 days. This is the time a man would require to traverse the distance covered; but it was completed

11 J.E. Rodó—*Bolívar*.

by an army, fighting against nature and man, and conquering both. Immediately after the triumph of Boyacá, Bolívar sent troops to the different sections of Nueva Granada, and felt the satisfaction of repaying this country for what she had done when she placed in his hands the army with which he first achieved the freedom of Venezuela. In Bogotá, he obtained money and other[12] very important resources with which to continue the war in Venezuela. As elsewhere, he used his marvelous activity in the work of organization, and in conducting his armies on the field of battle. A great assembly of the most prominent men of Bogotá conferred upon him the title of Liberator of Nueva Granada, and bestowed the same title on all the men composing his army, each one of whom also received a cross of honor called the Cross of Boyacá. A Vice-President of Nueva Granada was appointed, General Francisco de Paula Santander, the man who had organized the troops which Bolívar joined when he invaded the viceroyalty. Bolívar considered all the inhabitants as citizens of Colombia, without asking questions about their previous conduct, and issued passports to those who cared to depart.

After Boyacá, the campaigns of Bolívar were very swift, very successful and on a very different footing from his past campaigns. His enemies henceforth had to give up calling him the chieftain of rebels and bandits, and to treat him as an equal. He, however, by word and act showed to the world that he was not their equal, but very far their superior. After Boyacá "victory is always true, and grows, and spreads as the waters of a flood, and from peak to peak of the Andes, each mountain is a milestone of triumph."[13]

The royalists retreated from Bogotá, and Sámano fled to Cartagena. As for Bolívar, he soon returned to Venezuela, leaving the business of Nueva Granada in the hands of Santander, recommending him to respect the rights of everyone, because, as he said, "Justice is the foundation of the Republic."

In Angostura, there had arisen dissensions, and opposition to the vice-president, and even to Bolívar, himself. Some wanted him to be treated as a deserter because he had undertaken the campaign of Nueva Granada without the permission of Congress; some pronounced him defeated; some declared that he was fleeing to safety. Mariño, who had been called to occupy his seat in Congress, seconded by Arismendi, was the center of ill feeling against Bolívar. The vice-president was forced to resign, and Arismendi was elected in his stead. His first action was to appoint Mariño head of the army of the East. The substitution of a military president for a civilian was a vicious precedent which, unfortunately, has been followed in many instances by the Spanish American countries.

12 J.E. Rodó—*Bolívar*.
13 J.E. Rodó—*Bolívar*.

Arismendi proved, nevertheless, a good vice-president, and retained the cabinet appointed by Bolívar. Affairs were in this condition when news arrived of Bolívar's victory in Boyacá.

The Liberator had learned of the disturbances in Angostura on his way to Venezuela. He received also at this time the distressing news of the execution, ordered by Santander, of Barreiro and the other Spanish prisoners taken in Boyacá. Bolívar had proposed to the viceroy an exchange of prisoners, but the viceroy had not even answered Bolívar's communication. The Liberator had never agreed that the cause of freedom should be stained by the blood of prisoners, except in those very exceptional cases, already mentioned, when the War to Death decree was in effect. On some occasions, individual chieftains had not hesitated to commit crimes as heinous as those of the royalists. Though at times Bolívar had to ignore such actions, lest he be left alone by his followers, whenever he could prevent them, he did. He had recommended justice to Santander, who, though otherwise a distinguished officer, an able general and patriot, marred the fame he had acquired by this stupid act of cruelty, an act not to be justified even by the fact that Barreiro had ordered, without any form of law, the execution of many prisoners of war. Once, when a priest was imploring that the lives of prisoners be spared, Barreiro answered: "I am shooting them as I should shoot Bolívar were he ever to fall into my hands." Santander published a proclamation in which he tried to vindicate his conduct, but history has been just in its severity, condemning him unreservedly.

Once back in Angostura, Bolívar feigned ignorance of what had happened, and comported himself with much prudence and circumspection. Arismendi presented his resignation with words of modesty, and promises which he fulfilled thereafter. On December 14, Bolívar appeared before the Congress, and in an address gave a short report of his victory in Nueva Granada, voicing his constant aspiration for the union of Venezuela and Nueva Granada to form the republic of Colombia. He said:

"Its aspiration (that of Nueva Granada) to join its provinces to those of Venezuela is ... unanimous. The New Granadians are entirely convinced of the enormous advantages which would result to both countries from the creation of a new republic composed of these two nations. The union of Nueva Granada and Venezuela is the only purpose I have had since my first battles; it is the wish of the citizens of both countries, and it is the guaranty of the freedom of South America.... It behooves your wisdom to decree this great social act and to establish the principles of the pact on which this great republic is to be founded. Proclaim it before the whole world, and my services will be rewarded."

The vice-president endorsed the proposition of Bolívar with eloquent words, incidentally praising the victorious general and his troops. Among the persons who came to compliment him was an old foe named Mariano Montilla, a colonel in the army. Bolívar knew well how to discover real qualifications even in the hearts of his enemies, and he availed himself of this opportunity to establish strong bonds of friendship between himself and his former foe. He gave Montilla full powers to go to Cartagena, still in the hands of the Spaniards, with instructions to take it. Montilla proved worthy of Bolívar's trust. After fourteen months' siege, he captured Cartagena, as we shall see later.

On the 17th of December, 1819, Congress decreed the creation of Colombia by the union of Venezuela, Nueva Granada and Quito into a single republic. Bolívar was then elected president. Don Antonio Zea was elected vice-president for Venezuela, and Santander for Nueva Granada (also called Cundinamarca). No vice-president was elected for Quito. The organization of Quito was deferred until the army of freedom should enter that city.

The dream of Bolívar had come true again, and his prophecy made in Jamaica in 1815 had become a reality.

CHAPTER XIII

1820: HUMANIZING WAR. MORILLO'S WITHDRAWAL.

Meanwhile, in Spain, a great expedition was being prepared to come to America, an expedition which was intended to surpass even the army of Morillo. Fernando VII was determined to reëstablish his absolute power, not only in Spain but in the colonies. Morillo, in Venezuela, was asking for reinforcements. In his pleas for more men he stated that he wanted them to conquer Bolívar, "an indomitable soul, whom a single victory, the smallest, is enough to make master of 500 leagues of territory." Fernando VII was very willing to send this expedition, not merely to support his authority, but also to get rid of many officers who were accused of liberal principles. The army, gathered in Cádiz, was very soon undermined by subversive ideas. An officer named Rafael Riego led the insurrection, and on New Year's Day, 1820, instead of being on its way to America, the army was in revolt in the name of constitutional freedom. The ultimate result of this was that the expedition did not sail, and that Fernando VII had frankly to accept a constitutional program. Although Morillo endeavored to convey the idea that the events in Cádiz had little importance, the news which reached Bolívar after some delay strengthened his hope, for it seemed evident that Spanish soldiers were unwilling to come to America to fight against the insurgents.

In January, 1820, Bolívar again crossed the plains, where Páez was in command, and journeyed towards Bogotá, with the object of publishing the law establishing the Republic of Colombia. It was proclaimed there with solemnity by Santander, who, on communicating the event to the President, praised the latter with the following words: "Colombia is the only child of the immortal Bolívar." In March Bolívar was in Bogotá, where he gave the final orders for the various military operations to be conducted in the North and South.

In his absence, the Congress of Angostura decreed that he should use the official title *Libertador* before the word *Presidente*, and consider this title as his own on all occasions of his life. Many other honors were conferred upon him and his men. Grateful at heart, Bolívar devoted his attention to the stupendous task of organizing the country.

Meanwhile, Morillo, waiting for the Spanish reinforcements which never arrived, distributed his armies on the plains and in the southwest, in order to be in a position to fight Bolívar whenever the opportunity occurred. There were still nearly 15,000 men under Morillo, besides those who were in Nueva Granada occupying Cartagena and other smaller places, and those in possession of Quito. Bolívar organized another army, determined to try his forces once more against those of his powerful foe.

As a result of the revolution in Spain, Morillo had to proclaim and swear to the Spanish constitution in the provinces that he governed. This fact wrought a marked change in the position of the contending armies. The representative government established certain rights for provinces, and at the same time created the hope among the Spaniards that the revolution would end by conferring the privilege of representation on the American colonies.

The Spanish government initiated peace negotiations with the patriots, and Morillo was made president of a commission which went to talk this matter over with the heads of the Colombian revolution in July, 1820. A "Junta Pacificadora," or assembly to establish peace, was set up by Morillo in Caracas. Its first work was to send communications to the various generals to suspend military operations for a month, while settlement was being reached, and Bolívar was approached. On this occasion, Bolívar was addressed as "His Excellency, the President of the Republic." He was no longer the rebel, the insurgent or the bandit.

Bolívar was not to be deceived by any conciliatory attitude on the part of the government. He decided that all his subordinate officers should furnish every means for the conferences with the royalists, but always on the basis of the independence of Colombia.

"It will never be humiliating," he wrote in a letter to one of his officers, "to offer peace on the principles established in the declaration of the Republic of Venezuela,[14] which ought to be the foundation of all negotiations; first, because it is ordered by a law of the Republic, and second, because it is necessary according to the nature and for the salvation of Colombia."

Consequently, Congress answered the commissioners who came to deal with Bolívar that the sovereign congress of Colombia would listen with pleasure to all the propositions of the Spanish government, provided they were founded on the acknowledgment of the sovereignty and independence of Colombia, and that it would not admit any departure from this principle, often proclaimed by the government and people of the republic.

Latorre, one of the most distinguished and gentlemanly of the Spanish commanders, sent a personal note to Bolívar, in which he expressed the hope that Bolívar would some day give him the pleasure of embracing him as his brother. Bolívar answered accepting the armistice, but

14 That of November, 1818.

reiterated that he would listen to no proposition not based on the independence of Colombia.

The proposal of the Spanish commanders was that the provinces should adopt the political constitution of the Spanish monarchy; the King would permit the present chieftains to retain command in the provinces they were then occupying for an indefinite time, but subordinate either to the general of the Spanish army or directly to the Spanish government. The representative of Bolívar, for Bolívar did not attend the meeting through necessities of the campaign, declined to accept the proposals, and added:

> "The champions of justice and liberty, far from feeling flattered by promises of unlimited command, feel insulted to see themselves identified with the low element which prefers to oppress and be powerful to the sublime glory of being the liberators of their country."

Meanwhile, the diplomatic representatives of Colombia were strengthening the credit of the country in London. The public debt was recognized and a system of payment was decided on. Colombia, whose freedom was not yet accepted by the world, had at the time better credit than that of some of the European countries. On the other hand, some diplomatic movements were badly conducted in Europe. The royalist system was so deeply rooted in the spirits of men that many did not hesitate to take steps to establish independent kingdoms in America, with European princes at their heads. As a matter of fact, at that time, the Spanish colonies, with the exception of Colombia, showed very marked monarchical tendencies.

Mexico had given indication of her desire for a Spanish prince, and at last fell into the hands of Iturbide. In Buenos Aires also, a monarch was wanted, and it is well known that San Martín, the hero of Argentina and Chile, was very much in favor of the monarchical system. Colombia alone continued to support Bolívar in his idea concerning the establishment and the conservation of the Repúblican system. It is true that Bolívar wanted a president for life and an hereditary senate, but these ideas were rejected by his fellow citizens. He defended them with great vigor, and, if we are to judge by the history of anarchy succeeded by long periods of tyranny through which many countries of Spanish America have passed, we may believe that Bolívar's ideas were based on a knowledge of all the weaknesses characteristic of the Spanish American people of his time. He wanted to live up to the lofty words of Henry Clay, who, in the House of Representatives of the United States, proposed that Colombia should be recognized as a free country, "worthy for many reasons to stand side by side with the most illustrious peoples of the world," a solemn utterance which had little weight at that time in the United States, but which showed for the first time in a semi-official way that the United States was taking notice of the important movement of the South.

Bolívar, after an expedition to inspect the military operations of his army, sent a communication to Morillo, notifying him that he was ready to communicate with him. In a later letter, he asked Morillo to give instructions to his commanders to enter into a treaty to regularize the war, the horrors and crimes of which up to that time had steeped Colombia in tears and blood. The first arrangement made by the commanders of both sides was the agreement to an armistice to last during six months, covering all Colombia, and designating the lines where the contending armies should stay. It was also agreed that a treaty would be drafted providing for the continuance of war in accordance with international law and the usages of civilized countries. The initiative for these improvements was due to Bolívar, who was also the author of the basis of the treaty proposed by the Colombian delegates. Among the clauses of this agreement were some providing for the safety, good-treatment and exchange of prisoners; the abolition of capital punishment against deserters apprehended in the ranks of the enemy; the inviolability of lives and property in the sections tentatively occupied by the troops of the two armies; and the burial or incineration of the bodies of the dead on the field of battle. No treaty of the same nature entered into before that time had been so advanced in character. As Bolívar had previously said, the Venezuelans had nothing to lose; they had lost everything already; but the new treaty prevented further misfortune or abuse.

Subsequent to the signing of the treaty, Morillo expressed a desire to meet Bolívar personally, and Bolívar agreed. The two met in a town called Santa Ana, accompanied by a very few officers. Latorre also attended the meeting, but the presence of officers particularly distasteful to Bolívar was prevented by Morillo. Each of these two men represented in its noblest aspect the cause which he defended. It is strange that neither of them seemed to have been prepared by circumstances of early life for the role he was playing. Morillo was born of humble parentage, and from the lowest rung of the ladder he climbed to the highest place in the army, always in defense of the monarchy, until he received the titles of Count of Cartagena and Marquis of La Puerta; Bolívar, born in wealth, destined to become a millionaire and to be the recipient of every honor if he remained on the side of the oppressors of his country, sacrificed everything, lost his personal property to the last penny, and shared privations of every kind with his soldiers. When he had money, he gave it away; when he had no money, he gave away his food and clothing. His generosity was unlimited. On one occasion, when he learned that the man who had helped him to secure a passport after the surrender of Miranda was in prison and his estate about to be confiscated, Bolívar immediately asked that his own private property be taken instead of that of his friend.

But both Bolívar and Morillo were very much above the common chieftains, the bloodthirsty Boves, the ignorant Páez. They were the best representatives of what was truest and loftiest in Spanish power and in independent energy.

The interview was cordial. The two men embraced one another, had a long friendly conversation, and parted with a high mutual regard. They decided that a monument should be erected to commemorate their meeting. Bolívar's toast at a dinner tendered him on that occasion indicated clearly how he desired the war to be fought in the future. Lifting his glass, he said:

> "To the heroic firmness of all the fighters of both armies; to their constancy, endurance and matchless bravery; to the worthy men who support and defend freedom in the face of ghastly penalties; to those who have gloriously died defending their country and their government; to the wounded men of both armies who have shown their intrepidity, their dignity and their character ... eternal hatred to those who desire blood and who shed it unjustly."

Morillo answered in these words:

> "May Heaven punish those who are not inspired with the same feelings of peace and friendship that animate us."

From that day on the correspondence between the two men was very respectful and cordial.

Morillo knew well that he could not conquer the independent army, and he decided to return to Spain before he had lost his reputation in Venezuela. He asked to be recalled, and was succeeded by D. Manuel de Latorre, of whom we have already made mention. Transfer of the command was effected on the fourteenth of December, 1820.

CHAPTER XIV

1821: THE SECOND BATTLE OF CARABOBO. AMBITIONS AND REWARDS. BOLÍVAR'S DISINTERESTEDNESS. AMERICAN UNITY.

Sucre had been placed by Bolívar in command of the army of the South, with instructions to go to Guayaquil,—a section which was not covered by the armistice,—in order to negotiate its incorporation with Colombia. San Martín desired to have the province of Quito form part of Perú, and there is no ground for believing that he did so without sound and patriotic reasons. Bolívar, on his part, insisted that Quito and Guayaquil should belong to Colombia. Sucre had a very delicate mission, for he represented a man totally opposite in ideas to San Martín, although inspired by the same lofty motives and with the same noble purpose of freedom. Sucre went by sea to Guayaquil and prevented its invasion by the royalists, who had Quito in their possession.

Meanwhile, new commissioners came from Spain to undertake peace negotiations. On that occasion Bolívar wrote a very courteous letter to Latorre; and in a private communication he sent these friendly words to him:

> "I feel happy, my dear General, at seeing you at the head of my enemies, for nobody can do less harm and more good than you. You are destined to heal the wounds of your new country. You came to fight against it, and you are going to protect it. You have always shown yourself as a noble foe; be also the most faithful friend."

He also sent commissioners to Spain with a very polite and cordial letter to Ferdinand VII, so as to do his best to obtain the freedom of Colombia and its acceptance by Spain, avoiding, if possible, further fighting.

Maracaibo, which, as we have seen, had always been a royalist city, also decided to break with Spain; on this occasion, Latorre thought that Bolívar had broken the armistice, a thing that Bolívar denied, for he had not intervened in the movement, although he was ready to support the city in its labors towards freedom. He was willing to submit the decision of the question to arbitration, but Latorre did not acquiesce. Bolívar then notified him that hostilities were resumed. He was convinced that the Spanish Government never thought seriously of granting peace to the former colonies through accepting their independence. He immediately concentrated his forces, organized an expedition against Maracaibo, called the cavalry, ordered invasion of the province of Caracas, obtained incorporation of Páez and his plainsmen, and advanced towards the enemy. On opening the campaign, he published a proclamation offering pardon to the Spaniards and promising to send them to their country, and in all respects to obey the treaty on regularization of warfare. He also ordered his soldiers to obey the stipulations of that treaty.

> "The Government," he said, "imposes on you the strict duty of being more merciful than brave. Any one who may infringe on any of the articles on the regulation of war will be punished with death. Even when our foes would break them, we must fulfil them, so that Colombia's glory may not be stained with blood."

It must not be forgotten that these enemies of Bolívar were very different from the murderers commanded by Yáñez or Boves.

The new Colombian Congress convened in the city of Rosario de Cúcuta. Bolívar, as usual on such occasions, submitted his resignation in order to leave the Congress free to give the command to whomever it might select. Among the members of the Congress there were some men openly hostile to Bolívar, and in his communication he not only presented the usual reasons for resigning, but also stated frankly that he was tired of hearing himself called tyrant by his enemies. The Congress answered very cordially, asking him to remain in his position and assuring him of the gratitude of the Assembly for his valor and constancy.

Knowing that Latorre had advanced to Araure, the General moved with his army towards the town of San Carlos, where he received some reinforcements. As other independent commanders were harassing Latorre at different points, the Spaniard had to send some of his troops to repel these attacks, and so was forced to weaken his own army. Then he placed himself on the plain of Carabobo, where Bolívar, in 1814, had defeated the royalists commanded by Cagigal and Ceballos. There he was attacked by Bolívar on June 24, 1821. At eleven o'clock in the morning the battle began, and it developed with the swiftness of lightning. In an hour the royalist army was destroyed, not without great losses to the independents. In one hour not only the royalist army was defeated, but the Spanish domination in Venezuela had come to an end. In this battle, a very decisive rôle was played by the British legion, and by the brave *llaneros* commanded by Páez.

As the battle of Boyacá practically secured the independence of Nueva Granada, the battle of Carabobo secured the independence of Venezuela. Boyacá and Carabobo were up to that moment the greatest titles of glory for Bolívar, but his work was not completed, and America had still more and brighter glory in store for him. He, in his vigorous style, described the battle in a communication to the Congress, in which he said, among other things:

> "Yesterday the political birth of the Republic of Colombia was confirmed by a splendid victory."

Then he praised Páez, whom he immediately promoted to the rank of full General of the Army, and paid last homage to General Cedeño, who died in action,—

> "none braver than he, none more obedient to the Government ... He died in the middle of the battle, in the heroic manner in which the life of the brave of Colombia deserves to end....
>
> "The Republic suffers an equal pain in the death of the most daring Colonel Plaza, who, filled with unparalleled enthusiasm, threw himself against an enemy battalion to conquer it. Colonel Plaza deserves the tears of Colombia ... The Spanish army had over 6,000 picked men. This army does not exist any more; 400 of the enemy's men entered Puerto Cabello today."

The struggle for Venezuelan independence opened on April 19, 1810, in Caracas, and closed on June 24, 1821, at Carabobo.

The Congress decreed the highest honors to the conquerors of Carabobo, ordered a day of public rejoicing throughout the whole country, and set the following day for the funerals of all those who had fallen on the field of battle.

After the battle of Carabobo, Venezuela was divided into three military districts, which were placed under the command respectively of Mariño, Páez and Bermúdez, who had also been promoted to the rank of general. In this way, Bolívar tried to satisfy the ambitions of his officers, who, in more than one respect, considered their conquests as private property.

This was especially true of Páez. The Liberator had to be very careful in dealing with them, constantly impelled by the fear that through peace their restlessness would become a danger to the stability of the country. Bolívar summarized the situation when he exclaimed:

> "I am more afraid of peace than of war!"

His attention was then turned to the campaign of the South. He had been informed that San Martín was inclined to deal with the royalists, and he wanted to hasten there to avoid any such compromise. At this time he learned that the independence of Mexico was a fact, and he became impatient to finish the emancipation of Colombia by means of the freedom of the Isthmus of Panamá, which he used to call the "carrier of the universe."

Upon the organization of Colombia, as a result of the union of Nueva Granada and Venezuela, Bolívar was made president, and in that capacity he signed the constitution of 1821. In his communication to the Congress of Rosario de Cúcuta, he reiterated his desire to resign the command. On this occasion, his declaration could not be more emphatic.

> "A man like me is a dangerous citizen in a popular government. He is an immediate threat to the national sovereignty. I want to be a citizen in order to secure my own freedom and the freedom of everybody else. I prefer the title of citizen to that of Liberator, because the latter comes from war and the former comes from the law. Change, I beg you, all my titles for that of *good citizen*."

Of course, no one would think of accepting his resignation at a moment when his genius was most needed for the organization of the country.

We have mentioned very often the resignation of the Liberator from his command, and the invariable nonacceptance of it. Some enemies of Bolívar have declared that he never resigned in earnest, and have gone so far as to pronounce him an ambitious man who wanted all glory and power in Colombia and South America. The declarations made by Bolívar were made before the whole world. He had gained sufficient glory to be termed a great man, even though he left the army. If his resignation had been accepted, it is absolutely certain that he would have abandoned the power in order to keep untainted his reputation as a warrior, as an organizer, and as a self-sacrificing patriot. At that time he was praised by the North American press, as well as by men in every part of the world. The press of the United States opposed his resignation, considering it premature. General Foy said:

> "Bolívar, born a subject, freeing a world, and dying as a citizen, shall be for America a redeeming divinity, and in history the noblest example of greatness to which a man can arrive."

The Archbishop of Malines, Monsignor de Pradt, said:

> "The morality of the world, weakened with so many examples of violence, baseness, ambition, covetousness and hypocrisy, was in need of a stimulus like Bolívar, whose moderation and whose unheard-of abnegation in the full possession of power have rendered ambition hateful. The example of this great, virtuous man may serve as a general purification, strong enough to disinfect society."

The author of this monograph has been very keen to find all papers and documents in which appears disparaging criticism of the life of Bolívar.

He declares that he has never found one which is not invalidated by reasons of personal interest, political antagonism or prejudice. Bolívar's life was always consistent with his words. He was a man of power. Whenever occasion demanded it, he became a real dictator. At times necessity made him rather weak in dealing with the stormy elements of his own party, and only in exceptional circumstances, as in the sad case of General Piar did he rise to the plane of severity in letting justice take its course. A careful study of the life of Bolívar has produced a great change in the mind of the author of this work. He has come to realize that he was studying not merely the life and deeds of a great American, or even of a great man among all men, but the history of one of those exceptional beings selected by God to perform the highest missions and to teach great lessons. The student, upon leaving the subject, feels the same reverence experienced upon leaving a sacred place, where the spirit has been under the influence of the supernatural. Bolívar's ambition was the legitimate desire for glory, but he never wanted that power which consists in the oppression of fellowmen and the acquisition of wealth.

We have seen that General Sucre had gone by sea to Guayaquil, while Bolívar decided to go by land to Quito. He considered this campaign as decisive, but while he was making his preparations, he did not neglect the diplomatic relations of his country, the organization of finance nor the domestic service. He continued to dream of the unity of America. He never succeeded in attaining it, but that dream was the star to which he had hitched his chariot. He had been in communication with the statesmen of Argentina and Chile, and, as we have seen, in his proclamation sent to the inhabitants of Nueva Granada he expressed a desire that the motto of America should be "Unity in South America." He sent one plenipotentiary to Mexico, and another to Perú, Chile and Argentina. In his instructions to the latter he said the following words, which sound today, a century later, as though they had been uttered yesterday:

> "I repeat that of all I have expressed, there is nothing of so much importance at this moment as the formation of a league truly American. But this confederation must not be formed simply on the principles of an ordinary alliance for attack and for defense; it must be closer than the one lately formed in Europe against the freedom of the people.
>
> "It is necessary that our society be a society of sister nations, divided for the time being in the exercise of their sovereignty, on account of the course of human events, but united, strong and powerful, in order to support each other against aggressions of foreign powers.
>
> "It is indispensable that you should incessantly urge the necessary to establish immediately the foundations of an amphictyonic body or assembly of plenipotentiaries to promote the common interests of the American states, to settle the differences which may arise in the future

> between peoples which have the same habits and the same customs, and which, through the lack of such a sacred institution, may perhaps kindle deplorable wars, such as those which have destroyed other regions less fortunate."

In the projected treaty carried by the same representative, the following appears:

> "Both contracting parties guarantee to each other the integrity of their respective territories, as constituted before the present war, keeping the boundaries possessed at that time by each captaincy general or viceroyalty of those who now have resumed the exercise of their sovereignty, unless in a legal way two or more of them have agreed to form a single body or nation, as has happened with the old captaincy general of Venezuela and the kingdom of Nueva Granada, which now form the Republic of Colombia."

Similar instructions were given to the representative sent to Mexico.

The treaty arranged with Perú was similar to another entered into afterwards with Chile. In both documents it was stipulated: that an assembly should be organized with representatives of the different countries; that all the governments of America, or of that part of America which had belonged to Spain, should be invited to enter into that union, league, or perpetual confederation; that the assembly of plenipotentiaries should be entrusted with the work of laying the foundation for, and of establishing, the closer relations which should exist among all of those states; and that this assembly should "serve them as a council in great conflicts, as a point of contact in the common dangers, as faithful interpreter of their public treaties when difficulties occur, and as an arbitral judge and conciliator in their disputes and differences." In this way, two great principles were sanctioned by Bolívar: the principle of *uti-possidetis* and the principle of arbitration, which was proclaimed in America, for the first time, by Bolívar as president of Colombia.

Before leaving for the campaign of the South, the Libertador Presidente received the good news of Cartagena's fall into the hands of Montilla after fourteen months of siege, and of the insurrection of Panamá, which became independent and formed the eighth department of Colombia.

The importance of the independence of Panamá cannot be exaggerated. Bolívar wisely deemed it of greatest moment, and what has occurred during the twentieth century has proved that Bolívar was absolutely right in his judgment.

CHAPTER XV

1822: BOMBONÁ AND PICHINCHA. THE BIRTH OF ECUADOR. BOLÍVAR AND SAN MARTIN FACE TO FACE.

In January, 1822, Bolívar was in Cali, assembling his army to invade Quito by land.

This campaign proved to be the most difficult he had undertaken with respect to natural obstacles. Between Quito and his army, the Andes form a nucleus of mountains called the Nudo de Pasto. All the difficulties with which he had had to contend in the campaigns of Venezuela and Nueva Granada,—such as the flooded plains, the deep ravines between Venezuela and the Colombian valleys, the narrow and rugged passages, the wild beasts,—sink into nothingness as compared with the almost unconquerable obstacles which he was to face on his way to the South. In no other part of the continent do the Andes present such an appalling combination of ravines, torrents, precipitous paths and gigantic peaks. Furthermore, nowhere on the continent was the population so hostile to freedom as were the *pastusos* (inhabitants of the *Pastos*). Men, women and children cordially hated the cause of the Republic, and stopped at no crime to destroy the armies of Bolívar. Despite all this opposition, Bolívar made ready to throw the glories he had earned in Boyaca and Carabobo into the balance, risking everything to obtain the freedom of the peoples of the south, and the union of Quito and Colombia. This campaign presented difficulties greater than Napoleon himself ever found in his path. The Alps do not compare with these American mountains,—which rank with the Himalayas.

On the 8th of March, Bolívar began his advance to the South, being forced to leave a thousand men in the hospitals on the way. Scarcely two thousand men formed the army when it approached the formidable Nudo de Pasto. Sucre, who had been stationed in Guayaquil, moved so as to distract the attention of the Spaniards, thus helping Bolívar, and this was the only favorable circumstance.

Two thousand men were awaiting Bolívar in the city of Pasto, men who knew the country and who had the support of the inhabitants in their war against the independents. The commander of Pasto was a Spanish colonel named D. Basilio García.

The two armies met in a place called Bomboná, where all the advantages were on the side of the royalists. Bolívar found himself about to attack an army made almost invulnerable by nature; forests, roads, ravines—all protected it. In such a position, Bolívar merely said these words: "We must conquer and we will conquer!"

On the 7th of April the battle of Bomboná occurred. It lasted the entire afternoon and part of the night. The independent army rose to the occasion, and accomplished what it had never before realized. The light of the moon witnessed the retreat of the royalist army, defeated and destroyed, seeking shelter in the city of Pasto; and the name of Bomboná was written in history beside those of Boyacá and Carabobo as among the most momentous, the most significant battles fought for the cause of independence.[15]

The city of Pasto was unanimous against the Liberator, who now asked García to surrender. García at first refused, but finally accepted capitulation. He was a brave man and a creditable representative of Spanish heroism.

Bolívar entered Pasto. He was in such grave danger from the hostility of the inhabitants that he had to be escorted by Spanish soldiers, who, in this way, displayed their loyalty to their word and their high sense of honor.

This occurred on the 8th of June, 1822. The battle of Bomboná had taken place two months before, and in the interval another great event occurred in favor of the independent army. General Sucre, who had come to help Bolívar in the movement, had taken several cities as he advanced towards Quito. On the 24th of May he fought a decisive battle on the volcanic mountain of Pichincha, by which the independence of Quito was secured. The battle of Pichincha made Sucre the greatest general in the Repúblican army, after Bolívar. He captured 1,200 prisoners, several pieces of field artillery, guns and implements of war, and even made prisoner the Spanish commander, Aymerich. On the 25th of May, Sucre entered the city of Quito, two hundred and eighty years after the Spaniards arrived in that city for the first time.

With Sucre in Quito and Bolívar in Pasto, many bodies of royalist troops surrendered.

In the United States, the question of recognizing the independence of the South American countries finally came before Congress. On March 8,

---

15 Before the battle, General Pedro León Torres misunderstood an order from Bolívar. The latter instructed him to surrender his command to a colonel. Torres took a rifle and answered:

> "Libertador, if I am not good enough to serve my country as a general, I shall serve her as a grenadier."

Bolívar gave him back his command; Torres ordered the advance of his men and threw himself against the enemy, falling fatally wounded.

1822, with James Monroe as President and John Quincy Adams as Secretary of State, the ideas expressed by Henry Clay in 1820 were carried to full fruition. The press had been working in favor of independence, and the message of Monroe in favor of recognition was an interpretation of public opinion at that time. In the report presented to Congress was the following expression:

> "To deny to the peoples of Spanish America their right to independence would be in fact to renounce our own independence."

The independence of the South American countries was recognized by a congressional vote of 159 out of 160. It is better to forget the name of the man who opposed it. Spain fought against this measure but still it held. Colombia, Mexico and Buenos Aires entered into the concert of free nations.

Bolívar proceeded to organize the province of Los Pastos, and, with the help of the Bishop of Popayan,—a former foe to the cause of independence, who had wanted to return to Spain when the insurgents took possession of the city, but who was persuaded to remain by the noble words of Bolívar—finally obtained the consolidation of the republic in that section. A few days later Bolívar left Los Pastos for Quito, where he was received in triumph. The authorities of the old kingdom of Quito declared the city's desire to be reunited with the Republic of Colombia,—to become a part of the latter. Upon receiving the minutes of the assembly in which this decision was taken, Bolívar decided that this resolution should be placed before the proper representatives of the people, so that it might be given greater emphasis by their approval.

In the organization of the country, Bolívar formed the department of Ecuador of three old provinces. Sucre, promoted to the rank of major general, was appointed governor of this department. Then Bolívar addressed a letter to San Martin, at that time Protector of Perú, telling him that the war in Colombia had come to an end and that his men were ready to go wherever their brothers would call them, "especially to the country of our neighbors to the South."

There was a serious problem to be solved in the South, and it had to be worked out in Guayaquil. Two great men were going to come face to face. It is necessary to study, even briefly, the personality of the other noted man of the South, General San Martín.

D. José de San Martín was born on the 25th of February, 1778, of Spanish parents, in the little village of Yapeyú, in the missions established among the Indians in the northeast part of what is now the Argentine Republic. His father was lieutenant governor of the department. José was educated in Spain among youths of noble birth. At eleven years of age he entered the army. He fought in Africa, against the French, and in Portugal. In the campaign in Portugal he was a brother-in-arms of don Mariano Montilla, the hero of Cartagena. He rose to the position of lieutenant colonel. In 1811 he met Miranda in London, and then decided to come to Buenos Aires. He arrived there in 1812, and placed himself at the disposal of the revolutionary government, which gave him the grade of lieutenant colonel of cavalry. He immediately showed his talent as an organizer of men; he instructed his officers and disciplined his soldiers.

At the beginning of the Argentine revolution, the idea of independence was vague, and it was San Martín who first suggested that the revolutionists should call themselves "independents," so as to have a cause, a flag and principles by which they might be known. It is necessary to remember that the revolution in this section of America was always of a monarchical tendency, and San Martin was always an ardent supporter of monarchical ideas. The only battle in which he took part in Argentina was one in which he, with 120 men, defeated 250 foes. The independence of the viceroyalty of the River Plata caused very little bloodshed, except in the northern part, which is now the republic of Bolivia. San Martin was sent to fight the Spaniards in this section, but he well knew the futility of attacking by land, because the greatest stronghold of the Spaniards on the entire continent—the viceroyalty of Perú—was on the other side. He then feigned illness, and was sent as governor to the province of Cuyo, at the foot of the Andes, where he worked constantly and efficiently to organize a large army. He succeeded, not with the brilliancy of Bolívar's genius, but through the constancy of his own methodical soul.

San Martín was reserved. It was very difficult to know his thoughts and his feelings. He was successful in battle as well as in his deception of the enemy. In many respects he was the opposite of Bolívar.

In 1817 San Martín had 4,000 soldiers in Mendoza ready to invade Chile, where the insurgent armies had been defeated in Rancagua by a Spanish army sent from Perú. The remnants of the Chilean patriots dispersed, and some of them crossed the Andes and presented themselves to San Martín in the city of Mendoza. He received some and rejected others. Among the former was D. Bernardo O'Higgins, upon whose loyalty San Martín was certain he could depend.

San Martín crossed the Andes, and defeated the Spaniards at Chacabuco. Later, he fought the decisive battle of Maipó, passing then to Santiago, where he was proclaimed director of the state, from which position he immediately resigned, using all his influence to have O'Higgins appointed in his stead, which was done. O'Higgins was an honest man and an excellent administrator. He immediately appointed San Martín general-in-chief of the army, and together they planned the invasion of Perú by sea.

With the help of Admiral Cochrane, San Martín reached the shores of Perú, where he landed. After some delay, due to the desire to enlist public opinion in the cause of independence, he took the city of Lima on July 8, 1821, and was appointed Protector of Perú. He wished to unite Guayaquil and Perú, in which plan he was opposed by Bolívar.

Guayaquil had declared itself independent of Spain in October, 1820. We have seen that Sucre was sent there by Bolívar because that section had not been included in the armistice agreed to with Morillo in Santa Ana. In Guayaquil there were three parties, one on the side of Perú, one on the side of Colombia, and a third which desired the independence of that section. There were several movements in favor of and against these conflicting views, when Bolívar sent messages to Sucre, O'Higgins, San Martín, and other prominent men, in an endeavor to form a combination to bring about an early and successful end to the war for independence. In all the difficulties of Guayaquil, Sucre displayed exceptional prudence and tact, but when he was obliged to leave the city in order to draw to himself the attention of the Spaniards and thus facilitate the movement of Bolívar against Pasto, the intrigues increased, and Bolívar had to intervene, sending a message to the Junta of Guayaquil, asking them to recognize the union of Guayaquil and Colombia. San Martín was on the point of declaring war on Colombia, a fatal step which was prevented by the pressure of other more urgent matters, and perhaps because the victories of Bomboná and Pichincha were too recent to encourage any disregard of the conquerors.

As soon as Bolívar arrived in Quito, he decided to go to Guayaquil to take the situation in hand. He arrived on July 11, and was received in triumph, his presence producing a decided effect in favor of the union with Colombia. He published a proclamation inviting expressions of popular opinion as to union, and was waiting for the day on which the representatives of the province were to meet, when General San Martín appeared in the city, surprising everybody, for, although he had sent Bolívar a letter notifying him of his intended visit, Bolívar had not received it. He was most cordially received by the Liberator, who, in a previous communication, had declared his friendship for the Protector of Perú. San Martín landed on the 26th of July, and that night had a long personal conference with Bolívar, concerning which opinions varied. There were no witnesses of that interview. It is certain that the men discussed the union of Guayaquil, and the conflicting ideas of both leaders. Again the intellectual superiority of Bolívar was evident. One thing, however, is known: forty hours after landing in Guayaquil, the Protector left the city and went to Perú, where he resigned his position and then sailed for Chile, whence he went to the Argentine Republic. Later, he proceeded to Europe, where he died in the middle of the century, a great man, the victim of the ingratitude of his fellow citizens, always modest and reserved, and, in many respects, an unsolved mystery. He harbored no resentment towards Bolívar. When he arrived in Callao after the interview, the papers published the following words over his name:

> "The 26th of last July, when I had the satisfaction of embracing the Hero of the South, was one of the happiest days of my life. The Liberator of Colombia is not only helping this state with three of his brave battalions, united to the valiant division of Perú under the command of General Santa Cruz, to put an end to the war in America, but he is also sending a considerable number of arms for the same purpose. Let us all pay the homage of our eternal gratitude to the immortal Bolívar."

CHAPTER XVI

1822-1824: JUNÍN, A BATTLE OF CENTAURS. THE CONTINENT'S FREEDOM SEALED IN AYACUCHO.

After the victories of Bomboná and Pichincha Bolívar again evidenced his disinterestedness and his generosity in praising his officers. He reiterated his desire to resign his power. He expressed in a letter the need he felt for rest, and a belief that a period of repose might restore his former energy, which he felt slipping away from him.

Writing to a friend about Iturbide, he said:

> "You must be aware that Iturbide made himself emperor through the grace of Pío, first sergeant.[16] ... I am very much afraid that the four boards covered with crimson, and which are termed a throne, cause the shedding of more blood and tears and give more cares than rest.... Some believe that it is very easy to put upon one's head a crown and have all adore it; But I believe that the period of monarchy is passing and that thrones will not be up-to-date in public opinion until the corruption of men chokes love of freedom."

Regarding the battle of Pichincha, he said: "Sucre is the Liberator of Ecuador."

No better praise could be given his worthy lieutenant.

Once in Quito, he received the alarming news from Perú, which province had been left by San Martín, that several serious defeats had been suffered by the independents. He immediately made ready to free the viceroyalty from Spain, realizing that while Perú remained under Spain the independence of Colombia would be in danger. The viceroy of Perú had 23,000 European soldiers and all the resources necessary to carry on war.

Perú was the last South American country to proclaim its independence. Although there had been some movements of insurrection in 1809 in Alto Perú (now Bolivia), they were soon quelled and the country once more placed under the dominion of Spain. As a result, Perú was in position to send reinforcements to the royalists in Chile and was a constant menace to Colombia. The patriots of Chile, after obtaining their freedom, organized San Martín's expedition to invade Perú. When San Martín entered Lima early in July, 1821, the viceroy (Pezuela) was deposed by an assembly, and Laserna was appointed to take his place. Once in Lima,

---

16 Augustin de Iturbide was proclaimed Emperor of Mexico as the result of a mutiny led in Mexico City by a sergeant called Pio Marcha.

San Martín entered upon a period of inactivity which resulted in heavy losses to the independents. He was even ready to communicate with the Spaniards in order to arrange for the establishment of a regency in Perú, awaiting the arrival of a European prince to govern the country. He even appeared ready to go to Spain, himself, to beg for a prince.

The viceroy established his residence in Cuzco, the old capital of the Incas, and the Spanish officers obtained several partial victories.

The defeats of the independent forces brought about the dissolution of a *junta* which had taken charge of the government. At that time, Bolívar decided to intervene to help Perú gain her independence. He decided to send 3,000 men at once and to follow himself with 3,000 more to undertake this last part of his important work. As we have said, his decision in this matter was based, among other things, on the realization that the freedom of Colombia was in constant danger while the royalists occupied Perú. While making preparations for the campaign, he received news from Santander, the vice-president of Colombia, that the Spanish general, Morales, was advancing from Mérida to Cúcuta with a powerful army. He decided to send Sucre to Lima to handle the situation there and to go, himself, to Bogotá to defend his own country. He would have been unable to go to Lima immediately anyway, for he had not yet obtained permission from the Colombian government to do so. On his way to Bogotá he learned that the reports of the movements of Morales were very much exaggerated and that his forces were not so large as at first thought. Meanwhile, the Perúvians were insisting that Bolívar come to assist them, and the Constitutional Congress of Perú even instructed the President to ask the Libertador Presidente to inform his home government that the government of Perú ardently besought him to lend his assistance. Aware of the inefficient organization of the Peruvian forces, Bolívar strongly advised that attacks should not be made at once in order to see whether negotiations could bring about the desired results, or to allow time in which to improve the condition of the army.

He argued that no movement should be made until it was certain that independence could be gained only through the success of arms.

While Bolívar was still undecided, a powerful royalist army approached Lima, and the insurgents had to leave the capital and take shelter in the near-by port of Callao. Sucre, to whom the command of the united army had been offered, but who had not accepted this commission, directed the retreat. In Callao he assumed power, organized the insurgents of the city, and undertook other military operations. The royalists remained in Lima for a short while only, and then their opponents reoccupied the city.

Once more Bolívar was obliged to leave Guayaquil, this time to go to Quito to defend the city against the *pastusos*, who had again rebelled. After punishing them, he sent men to the city of Pasto to finish the work of pacification, and he returned to Guayaquil in January, 1823, where he was met by a commission sent from Perú to insist upon his taking command of the Perúvians. Upon receipt of authorization from the Colombian government, he proceeded to Callao, where he arrived on the first of September, 1823. Congress conferred upon Bolívar the title of Libertador, and placed in his hands supreme military authority over all the forces of the country. In order to insure close coöperation between the civil administration and the military operations, he was vested with political and executive authority. Bolívar accepted these powers with great modesty, and remarked:

> "I do for Perú more than my ability permits, because I count upon the efforts of my generous fellows-in-arms. The wisdom of Congress will give me light in the midst of the chaos, difficulties and dangers in which I see myself.... I left the capital of Colombia, avoiding the responsibilities of civil government. My repugnance to work in governmental affairs is beyond all exaggeration, so I have resigned forever from civil power so far as it is not closely connected with military operations. The Congress of Perú may count, nevertheless on all the strength of Colombian arms to give the country unlimited freedom. By protecting national representation I have done for Perú the greatest service a man could do for a nation."

There were elaborate festivities in honor of Bolívar, and his moderation, as well as his other personal qualifications, was recognized and admired. General O'Higgins of Chile was present on that occasion. At one of the banquets, Bolívar proposed a toast voicing the hope that the children of America might never see a throne raised in any of its territories, and that, as Napoleon was exiled in the middle of the ocean, and the new emperor, Iturbide, thrown out of Mexico, all usurpers of the rights of the people might fall, and that not one of them might remain throughout the New World.

Bolívar had many difficulties to overcome in the work of organizing the elements of the country for the final struggle. Perúvians had not been hardened by constant fighting as had Venezuelans and New Granadians, and although they were patriotic and anxious to obtain their freedom, yet they lacked the ardor that only Bolívar knew how to kindle in men's hearts. He decided to hasten the advance of the Colombian reinforcements, knowing that he could trust them to form a strong nucleus around which he could organize the Peruvian campaign. In the midst of his incessant work, he would say:

> "We must conquer or die! And we will conquer, for Heaven does not want us in chains."

In January, 1824, Bolívar became very ill with fever. Before he had fully recovered he began to direct the preparations for the campaign, and while convalescing displayed remarkable energy in his work.[17] At times, though, he showed some signs of discouragement. He had already said he felt that his energy was diminishing, and in a letter to General Sucre he wrote:

> "I am ready to meet the Spaniards in a battle to end war in America, but nothing more. I feel tired, I am old, and I have nothing to expect."

He had something to expect: the last and final victories, and then the ingratitude of his fellow citizens. Perhaps at that time he was beginning to feel the advances of the illness which caused his death.[18]

Then an event occurred which almost destroyed all of Bolívar's well-made plans. Some troops sent from the River Plata started a rebellion in Callao, and, before anything could be done to correct the situation, the Spanish flag was hoisted over the fortress and messages had been sent to the viceroy offering to deliver the city. Laserna sent General Rodil, appointing him governor and military commander of the province of Lima, and placing him in full command of the fortress and the treacherous soldiers. This was a severe loss for the Repúblican cause. Congress at once suspended the constitution and the law and appointed Bolívar dictator, for it realized that he was the only man to cope with the situation. The royalist army had 18,000 men, 12,000 to fight Bolívar, who was then in the city of Trujillo, and 6,000 to keep Upper Perú (now Bolivia) and the southern coast, subject to Spain. Bolívar had from 4,000 to 6,000 Colombians and about 4,000 Perúvians, all in poor condition. He gathered all the resources available in Lima, but desertion and treachery had left very little of use. At that time, to be disloyal was a fashionable thing for

---

17 When he was still very weak, sitting ghost-like in an armchair, his friend don Joaquín Mosquera, who had been his ambassador to the countries of the South, asked him, "And now, what are you going to do?" "To conquer," answered Bolívar.

18 Tuberculosis.

the insurgents of Lima. However, Bolívar would not despair. In a letter written at that time, he said:

> "This year will not come to a close without our having gained Potosí."

His chief hope had been in the army of Colombia; but, while in Trujillo, he learned that the government of Colombia would not send any troops or resources without express authorization from Congress, which meant a long delay. Meanwhile, the Spaniards under command of Canterac were advancing against Trujillo. Bolívar set to work again with that feverish activity which seemed to enable him to create everything from nothing—men, uniforms, arms, horses, even horseshoes. The smallest detail, near or at a distance, was the object of his care, and he attended to everything with that precision and accuracy which form a great proportion of what we call genius.

The city of Pasco was selected by Bolívar as the meeting place of all the independent forces, and the month of May chosen for the general movement. In June the Andes were crossed, and on August 2nd, the army was assembled on the plain of Sacramento, near Pasco. There he arranged his soldiers for battle and decided to attack on the 6th the royalists, who were near by. Canterac was approaching with an army of 9,000 of which 2,000 were cavalrymen.

On August 6, 1824, at four o'clock in the afternoon, the two armies met on the plain of Junín, near the lake of that name, the source of the Amazonas. This battle was one of cavalry only, and was in appearance and in results one of the most terrible. Throughout the whole combat not one shot was fired. Only the horsemen fought, but the defeated royalist cavalry on retreat, drew the infantry with them. The battle of Junín ranked in importance with those of Boyacá, Carabobo and Bomboná, as well as that of Pichincha, and had a marked effect on the ultimate success of the Peruvian campaign. The morale of the royalists was destroyed. Canterac, in his retreat, was forced to cover 450 miles of very rough country, and lost a large part of his army.

A festivity following this success was the occasion of generous words exchanged between the victor of Bomboná and the conqueror of Pichincha. Sucre said:

> "Led by the Liberator, we can expect nothing but victory!"

to which Bolívar answered:

> "To know that I will conquer, it is enough to know who are around me."

At another time, Bolívar reiterated his feelings in the following way:

> "Let the valiant swords of those who surround me pierce my breast a thousand times if at any time I oppress the countries I now lead to freedom! Let the authority of the people be the only existing power on earth! Let the name of tyranny be obliterated from the language of the world and even forgotten!"

Bolívar then left the army in the command of Sucre and departed for the seaboard to continue his work of organization.

The royalists had left Lima as soon as they learned of the defeat of Junín. Rodil was in the fortress at Callao. The viceroy in Cuzco gathered all the soldiers he could, forming an army of 11,000 men, and started out to avenge the defeat of Junín.

On December 9, 1824, the two armies met on the plain of Ayacucho, and at noon began the final battle of the Wars of Independence on the American continent. At first the Spaniards had some success. Then General Córdova of the army of Sucre, jumped from his horse, killed it with his sabre, and exclaimed to his soldiers: "I do not want any means of escape. I am merely keeping my sword to conquer. Forward, march of conquerors!" The royalists could not resist Córdova. They put all their reserves into action, but the soldiers of the independent army were determined to triumph, and Córdova, himself, had the glory of taking the viceroy prisoner. It is said that in the afternoon of that day the insurgents were fewer in number than their prisoners. A capitulation was proposed and was accepted, Canterac signing on account of the capture of the viceroy. The generals and officers promised not to fight any more in the War of Independence nor to go to any place occupied by royalists. Callao was included in the capitulation, but Rodil did not accept.

Bolívar possessed the virtue of creating heroes by his side: Anzoátegui in Boyacá; Páez in Carabobo; Torres in Bomboná; Sucre, commander-in-chief in Pichincha and Ayacucho; and Córdova, under Sucre's command, in the last fight for independence.

The War of Independence of Latin America began in Caracas on April 19, 1810, and ended in Ayacucho on December 9, 1824. Writing about this battle, Bolívar said:

> "The battle of Ayacucho is the greatest American glory and is work of General Sucre. Its arrangement was perfect; its execution superhuman. Swift and clever maneuvers destroyed in one hour the victors of fourteen years, and an enemy perfectly organized and ably commanded."

He conferred the highest honors on Sucre, and bestowed the titles of Grand Marshal and General, Liberator of Perú, on him. In a letter to Sucre, he wrote:

> "The ninth of December, 1824, when you triumphed over the foe of independence, will be remembered by countless generations, who will always bless the patriot and warrior who made that day famous in the annals of America. So long as Ayacucho is remembered, the name of Sucre will be remembered. It will last forever."

The battle of Ayacucho practically put an end to the War of Independence of America, which began with the battle of Lexington, April 19, 1775.

CHAPTER XVII

1825-1827: BOLIVIA'S BIRTH. BOLÍVAR'S TRIUMPH. THE MONARCHICAL IDEA. FROM HONORS TO BITTERNESS.

Immediately after Ayacucho, Bolívar ordered the cessation of conscription and called a constitutional convention for February 8, 1825.

> "The deplorable circumstances which forced Congress to create the extraordinary office of dictatorship have disappeared," he said, "and the Republic is now able to constitute and organize itself as it will."

Passing from national interests to his great idea of American union, he issued a circular to all the governments of the continent to carry into practice the assembly of plenipotentiaries of Latin America.

> "It is now time," he wrote, "that the common interests uniting the American republics had a fundamental basis to make permanent the duration of their governments, if possible. The task of establishing this system and affirming the power of this great political body must rest upon that lofty authority which may direct the policies of our governments and keep their principles of conduct uniform, an authority whose name alone will calm our storms. So respectable an authority can exist only in an assembly of plenipotentiaries, designated by each one of our republics and united under the auspices of the victory obtained by our armies against the Spanish government.... The day when our plenipotentiaries exchange their powers will start an immortal epoch in the diplomatic history of America. When, after one hundred centuries, posterity seeks the beginning of our international law, it will remember the agreements which affirmed its destiny and will gaze with respect upon the conventions of the Isthmus. And then it will find the plan of the first alliances showing the course of our relations with the world. What will the Isthmus of Corinth then be, compared with the Isthmus of Panamá?"

Bolívar now sent his resignation to Colombia, stating that since he had fulfilled his mission and there were no more enemies in America, it was time to carry out his promise. At this very time he was beginning to be attacked by his enemies as an ambitious man who desired monarchial power! These attacks, it was clear to him, would become more numerous, and even foreigners would take part in the abuses. But there does not now exist one document which warrants a single accusation against Bolívar for immoderate aspirations.

When the War of Independence had practically come to a close Rodil was holding Callao, and Upper Perú was still in the hands of the Spanish.

Sucre undertook to remedy this situation while Bolívar attended to the convening of the constitutional congress in Perú. The Liberator remarked how dangerous it was "to put into the hands of any one man a monstrous authority which could not be placed without danger into the hands of Apollo himself." Speaking to the delegates he said he desired:

> "to compliment the people because they have been freed of that which is most dreadful in the world, war, through the victory of Ayacucho, and despotism, through my resignation. Proscribe forever, I pray you, such enormous authority, which was the doom of Rome. It was praiseworthy, undoubtedly, for Congress, in order to pass through the abyss and face terrific storms, to substitute the bayonets of the liberating for its laws, but now that the country has secured domestic peace and political freedom, it should permit no rule but the rule of law."

The Perúvians insisted that Bolívar should retain the power, and passed a decree conferring it on him, without, however, calling him dictator, so as to respect his will. On the same day a decree ordered several honors to be paid him and also that one million pesos (about $1,000,000) be distributed among the officers and soldiers of the liberating army, and that another million pesos be placed in the hands of the Liberator as a token of gratitude of the country.

Bolívar was very much moved, and, to a certain extent, hurt by this pecuniary reward. He declined to accept in the following words:

> "I have never wanted to accept, even from my own country, any reward of this kind. It would be a monstrous incongruity if I should receive from the hands of Perú that which I refused to receive from the hands of my country."

Congress finally asked Bolívar to take the million dollars and devote it to charities in his own country and other parts of the republic of Colombia. This Bolívar agreed to do.

Bolívar decided to remain in Perú until the convening of the following congress, which was to assemble in 1826. He immediately bent all his energy to the work of government, in which he was, if possible, more admirable than he was as a soldier. Among the several measures of his administrative work was the establishment of normal schools in the departments, tribunals of justice, several educational institutions, mining bureaus, roads, public charities and multitudinous other services.

On April 1, 1825, Sucre defeated the last Spanish troops in a place called Tumusla.

Upon the completion of his work, Bolívar started to visit Cuzco and Upper Perú. In the city of Arequipa, on May 16, he issued a decree proclaiming the republic of Alto (Upper) Perú. In Cuzco he was received in triumph. A thousand ladies offered him a beautiful crown set with pearls and diamonds. The Liberator received it and immediately sent it to Marshal Sucre, saying:

> "He is the conqueror of Ayacucho and the true liberator of this republic."

From Cuzco, Bolívar went to La Paz, and there he was received in like manner. The assembly of Alto Perù sent representatives to meet him. The country had received the name of República Bolívar (now Bolivia). From there he went to Potosí, where he remained several weeks, accepting the homage and gratitude of the people. There he received several members of the diplomatic corps and a committee sent by the government of Buenos Aires with the purpose of complimenting him for the services he had rendered to the cause of South American independence which, as they said, Bolívar had made secure forever.

He gave Bolivia its first political organization, applying his favorite ideas about the distribution of powers. Here he repeated what he had done everywhere when in command. He established educational institutions; ordered that the rivers be examined in order to study the feasibility of changing their courses so as to furnish water to arid and sterile areas; distributed land among the Indians; suppressed the duties on mining machinery; ordered the planting of trees, and showed in a thousand ways his untiring energy, all the while keeping in active diplomatic correspondence and in constant communication with his friends and civil officers, in order to give instructions in detail. He issued orders from Chuquisaca to have the Venezuelan soldiers sent back to their country from Perú. He even went so far as to entertain thoughts of the independence of Cuba and Porto Rico.

In January, 1826, he left Chuquisaca for the coast and from there he sailed for Perú, and a month later reached Lima, where he rendered an account of what he had done in Upper Perú and in the South. By that time the last stronghold of the Spaniards, Callao, had fallen into the hands of the Venezuelan general, Bartolomé Salom, a very distinguished officer who had played a remarkable rôle under Bolívar during the War of Independence. The resistance of Rodil in Callao is one of the best examples of Spanish bravery. Rodil was a rough soldier, and often harsh and cruel in his measures. In spite of hunger, illness and losses, he remained in Callao for almost eleven months, not surrendering until January 23, 1826; he and his men were the last representatives of the Spanish power to leave the continent.

As soon as everything was well organized in Perú, Bolívar made ready to return to Colombia. At that time some imprudent friends tried to convince him that it was to the best interest of the now independent countries that he should be made emperor of the Andes, which covered Colombia, Perú and Bolivia. From Caracas, Páez proposed that he should return to Colombia and set up a monarchy. Bolívar steadfastly refused to listen to any of these seductions. To Páez he wrote:

> "France had always been a kingdom. The Repúblican government discredited itself and became more and more debased until it fell into an abyss of hate. The ministers who led France were equally cruel and inept. Napoleon was great, singular, and, besides that, extremely ambitious. Nothing of the kind exists here. I am not Napoleon, no I wish to be; neither do I want to imitate Caesar, and still less Iturbide.... The magistrates of Colombia are neither Robespierre nor Marat.... Colombia has never been a kingdom. A throne would produce terror on account of its height as well as on account of its glamour."

To all his friends he declared his decided opposition to the monarchical idea. In another letter, addressed to vice-president Santander, he wrote:

> "I have fulfilled all my obligations, for I have done my duty as a soldier, the only profession which I have followed since the first day of the Republic.... I was not born to be a magistrate.... Even if a soldier saves his country, he rarely proves a good executive.... You, only, are a glorious exception to this rule."

One of the greatest rewards for his ambition, the one he valued the most throughout the rest of his life, was received at that time. It consisted of Washington's picture and a lock of his hair, sent as a present by Washington's family from Mount Vernon through General Lafayette. In his letter to Bolívar, Lafayette said:

> "My religious and filial devotion to General Washington could not be better recognized by his family than by honoring me with the commission they have entrusted to me.... Of all men living, and even of all men in history, Bolívar is the very one to whom my paternal friend w have preferred to send this present. What else can I say to the great citizen whom South America has honored with the name of Liberator, confirmed in him by two worlds, a man endowed with an influence equal to his self-denial, who carries in his heart the sole love of freedom and of the republic?"

Bolívar answered:

> "There are no words with which I can express how my heart appreciates this gift.... Washington's family honors me beyond my greatest

hopes, because Washington's gift presented by Lafayette is the crown of all human rewards."[19]

While yet aglow with the great satisfaction he derived from this episode, Bolívar was annoyed again by the movement to make him accept a crown. Something still worse occurred at this time. In 1826 trouble broke out in Venezuela because of the activities of Páez.

We have already mentioned that Venezuela was divided into three military districts, governed by Bermúdez, Mariño and Páez. These three men had been at times hostile to Bolívar, and, in order to satisfy their ambitions, he had placed them in high commands. Páez was stationed in Caracas, where his arbitrary rule was resented by the people. He intrigued against the vice-president, Santander, executing his commands in such a way as to produce ill-will, especially an order providing for the recruiting of soldiers in Venezuela, which because of the manner of its execution, caused much protest and resulted in complaints to the House of Representatives against Páez. The House endorsed the accusation and submitted it to the Senate, which suspended Páez from his post and summoned him to the capital. Páez refused to appear, but at last was obliged to leave his command and retire to Valencia as a private citizen. Once there, he instigated all sorts of disturbances, and succeeded in creating an appearance of popular clamor for his reinstatement in command of the department in order to avoid anarchy. In this he was helped by his friends and partisans. A faction asked him to accept the military command of the department, and Páez, supported by the municipal council of Valencia, did so in disobedience to Congress. He adopted the title of Military and Civil Chief of Venezuela. He succeeded in enlisting the support of Mariño, but not that of Bermúdez, in spite of all his flattering propositions. Thus started the endless chain of civil revolutions in independent Latin America.

Santander wrote to the Libertador asking him to help save the country from revolution. Páez also sent a communication to him, in which he complained against vice-president Santander. Bolívar decided to return at once to his country, but he met with strong opposition on the part of the Peruvian authorities and people. After some hesitation, he concluded to return home, thus ending the period which marks the height of his popularity. Soon his glory was to be tarnished by ingratitude. He departed from Perú never to return. "Whatever remains of that life is sorrow."[20]

19 From that time until his death Bolívar preferred to any other decoration, Washington's miniature picture, which often he wore on his breast. Venezuela keeps with veneration this sacred relic in the *Museo Boliviano* of Caracas.

20 Bolívar—J.E. Rodó.

On the way to his country, Bolívar found that the southern provinces of Colombia wanted him to be dictator, but he declared that it was his desire that the constitutional regime should continue. He sent a proclamation to the Colombians, once more offering his services as a brother.

> "I do not want to know," he said, "who is at fault. I have never forgotten that you are my brothers-in-blood and my fellow soldiers.... Let there be no more Cundinamarca; let us all be Colombians, or death will cover the deserts left by anarchy."

He crossed at the foot of the lofty Chimborazo and arrived in Quito, where he was again received with rejoicing, as he had been in all the towns on his way home; and again he was urged to assume dictatorship. This he steadfastly refused to do. In the middle of November he arrived in Bogotá, where he exhorted the people to union and concord. He expressed much satisfaction at the obedience to law on the part of the army, "because if the armed force deliberates, freedom will be in danger, and the mighty sacrifices of Colombia will be lost." For two days only he exercised the executive power, but those days were sufficient to deepen the impression he had left as a great organizer. He then continued on his way to Venezuela, learning that Páez, who was openly opposed to the most cherished ideas of Bolívar, had convoked a Venezuelan constitutional congress to meet in Valencia on the 15th day of January, 1827. Appreciating the type of man he was to face, Bolívar gathered a small army, to be prepared for contingencies. On his way he learned that Puerto Cabello, which had declared itself in favor of union, had been attacked by Páez and that Venezuelan blood had been shed. Upon his arrival at Maracaibo, he published a proclamation, resolved to make every effort at persuasion before resorting to the sword. Páez had declared that Bolívar was coming to Venezuela as a citizen to help with his advice and experience to perfect the work of reform. From Coro, the Libertador wrote him, attempting to convince him that his conduct was criminal and making him flattering offers if he would desist. When the people of Caracas learned that Bolívar was approaching, a reaction took place, to such an extent that Páez became frightened. Some of the population openly declared themselves in Bolívar's favor.

On the last day of 1826, Bolívar's mind passed through a crisis in an effort to decide what steps would best reduce Páez to obedience, and, if possible, avoid bloodshed. On the following day, the first of 1827, he issued a decree, by virtue of his extraordinary powers, granting an armistice to all those who had taken part in the so-called reform movement, and ordering that his authority as President of the Republic be recognized and obeyed. He also offered to convoke a national convention.

Páez hesitated no longer; he acknowledged the authority of Bolívar as President, annulled the decree convoking a congress, and ordered that the President should be honored in all the towns from Coro to Caracas. From Puerto Cabello, Bolívar issued a beautiful proclamation in which he said:

> "There are no longer any enemies at home.... Today peace triumphs.... Let us drown in the abyss of time the year 1826.... I have not known what has happened. Colombians, forget whatever you know of the days of sorrow."

Páez humiliated himself to the point of asking that he be tried, but Bolívar would not permit it. He even praised Páez for his self-denial, going so far in his generosity as to call him *savior of the country*. This generosity was censured, especially by the people of Nueva Granada, and was considered a weakness on the part of Bolívar. It was thought to be an indication that he feared his authority would not be sufficiently strong to carry him through the dangerous business of disciplining a man with so large a following as Páez. But this was not so. Bolívar had, upon the occasion of Piar's treachery, shown himself capable of decisive, if difficult action; but his preference was always for justice tempered with mercy. That he felt no weakening in personal power is shown by the following incident: At a banquet where Páez and his partisans formed the great majority of those present, a man started a debate which gave Bolívar opportunity to make very energetic declarations, and even to utter the following words:

> "Here is no other authority and no other power than mine. Among all my lieutenants I am like the sun; if they shine it is because of the light I lend them."

Silence followed these words; everybody, including Páez, realized that Bolívar could make himself respected whenever he wished.

His reception in Caracas surpassed any one that Bolívar had ever been given. He could not walk because of the crowd. He had to listen to addresses, hymns and eulogies, receive crowns, attend banquets and accept all kinds of homage. His modesty was recognized by an inscription on one of the banquet tables: "To conquer in the field of battle may be the work of fortune; to conquer the pride of victory is the work of the conqueror." Páez, who had been presented a sword by Bolívar, expressed his gratitude in the warmest terms, and pledged himself to the service of his fellow citizens.

> "I should rather die a hundred times," he said, "and lose every drop of my blood than to permit this sword to leave my hand, or ever attempt

to shed the blood which up to now it has set free.... Bolívar's sword is in my hands. For you and for him I shall go with it to eternity. This oath is inviolable."

CHAPTER XVIII

1828: THE CONVENTION OF OCAÑA. FULL POWERS. AN ATTEMPT AT MURDER.

It was Bolívar's fortune to dispel the effect of evil with his presence, but in his absence evil was certain to raise its head. While he triumphed in Caracas, he was being severely criticised in Bogotá, even by Santander. His generosity with regard to Páez irritated the people of Nueva Granada to the extreme.

When Congress convened, Bolívar tendered his resignation, as usual, but this time he insisted still more. "For fourteen years," he wrote, "I have been Supreme Chief and President of the Republic. Danger forced me to accept this duty. Now that the danger has passed, I may retire to enjoy private life." The rest of his communication evidenced the sincerity of his desires and his modesty. He finished with these words: "I implore of Congress and of the people the grace to be permitted to resume my simple citizenship."

In spite of the resignation, intrigues continued in Nueva Granada, and the separatist feeling grew stronger and stronger in that country and in Venezuela. Through the separation of Nueva Granada, Bolívar's enemies in that nation saw a way to get rid of him without displaying their enmity, since, being a citizen of Venezuela, Bolívar could not be president of Nueva Granada. Páez and his partisans, on their side, did not want to have Santander in authority, because Santander was not a native of Venezuela. The situation was made more complicated and more serious by a rebellion in Lima, followed by another in Guayaquil. Notwithstanding that his resignation had been tendered, Bolívar, considering that the union of Colombia was threatened, immediately started for Bogotá, to take the situation in hand. He resolved to sacrifice everything to prevent anarchy from taking the place of freedom and mutiny from taking the place of law. He left Caracas, his native city, and here again he was taking a last farewell. In July he was in Cartagena, where the people received him with genuine affection. He recalled that it was from here he had begun his first quixotic expedition to his country in 1812. Fifteen years had elapsed since then, and he was again in Cartagena, his great work of redemption fulfilled but now in danger of being destroyed.

The steps taken by the Liberator to organize the attack against the revolutionists were described by Santander and his followers as steps to destroy the country and its political freedom. It was publicly proposed that Nueva Granada should declare null the fundamental convention providing for the union of the country with Venezuela. Santander was ready to begin the work of resistance. He was persuaded to be prudent, but not before he had given vent to his immoderate anger in ignoble expressions. He went so far as to state that war should be declared against Bolívar, for, if they were to be deprived of public liberty, it would have been better, he said, to remain under Spain. Morillo was to him preferable to Bolívar.

Bolívar advanced towards Bogotá. Santander endeavored to stop him, sending him word that the army was not necessary since constitutional order had been reestablished in Guayaquil. Bolívar knew better, and continued his advance. On the 10th day of September he arrived in Bogotá, was received by the Congress, took the oath of office and delivered an address in which he offered to govern according to the constitution, in order to keep Colombia free and united until the meeting of the national convention. Santander greeted Bolívar formally. They had a long conversation in which the Liberator showed unbounded generosity.

Congress had entire confidence in Bolívar. It approved all the steps he had taken and gave him powers to execute other measures seemingly necessary to the life of the Republic. It also issued a communication providing for a general convention in the city of Ocaña on the 2nd of March, 1828. This convention was the last hope for the reestablishment of the Republic. Bolívar recommended that, in the election of representatives, the people select honorable men, possessed of intense patriotism and devotion to the independence, union and freedom of Colombia. He sent a request to Guayaquil not to leave the Union, and he had the satisfaction of learning that a counter revolution had put an end to the work of secession in that section of the country. Other minor movements were soon defeated and an alarm over a reported Spanish invasion subsided.

The convention took place in Ocaña, and after the work of preparation it formally inaugurated its work on April 9th. Among its members were some of Bolívar's most bitter enemies, some of his closest friends and a group of so-called independents who were ready to swing to either side. The convention proved a field of discord and of disgraceful disputes. Bolívar experienced keen anguish at the thought of the inevitable results of the meeting of that ill-advised group of men, and feared that it would lead to anarchy. He sent a message in which he exhorted the convention to save Colombia from ruin and to give it security and tranquility. He demanded a firm, powerful and just government to indemnify her for the loss of 500,000 men killed in the field of battle.

> "Give us a government under which law is obeyed, the magistrate is respected, and the people are free; a government which can prevent the transgression of the general will and of the people's commands ... In the

> name of Colombia, I pray you to give us for the people, for the army, for the judge and for the magistrate an inexorable government."

Bolívar knew that in his appeals for a strong government his enemies would see, or pretend to see, personal ambitions, and Santander, of course, immediately exploited this feeling against him. But Bolívar, who had proved his disinterestedness when he might have had anything he desired, made no effort, at this time, when he was trying to rescue his country from grave danger, to show that he was not ambitious.

A large number of petitions were received by the general assembly, requesting that Bolívar continue in control of the government "as the only man who, because of his talents, his exceptional services and his powerful influence, can keep Colombia united and tranquil." But the convention was agitated by opposing feelings and influences. The federal system was proposed, but it was not accepted, although the proposal was greeted with joy by the enemies of the Liberator.

Bolívar, at about this time, wrote to a friend:

> "If the constitution to be adopted in Ocaña is not suitable to the situation in which I see Colombia, I shall abandon at once a government of which I am tired at heart."

And to his sister he wrote:

> "I have decided to leave for Venezuela, and I want you to know this, warning you that I absolutely do not want you, on your account or on mine, to incur the least expense, for you well know how poor I am."

And this was the man who had been born wealthy, who had declined to accept a million dollars from Perú, who gave his salary to the needy, who could have had all life can give, but who renounced all to devote himself to his country!

When the constitution was drafted, Bolívar found that it was going to be contrary to his desires, and he made ready to return to Venezuela, but was persuaded by the insistence of his friends to remain. At last, they, fearing the oppression of Santander and his followers, left Congress. This destroyed the quorum, as other representatives had already resigned. On June 11th, they issued a proclamation explaining the failure of the Congress, attributing it to the oppression by a party which desired a constitution unsuited to Colombia, and which overlooked the real facts of the situation; and declared that the legal status of the country was as follows:

> "The constitution of the year 1811 is in full vigor; the laws are in force, and at the head of the government is the Libertador Presidente, who has the confidence of the nation."

When Bolívar was informed that the convention had adjourned, he wanted to return to the capital and withdraw from public life. This would have meant civil war with no man powerful enough to put an end to it. In the emergency an assembly of respectable persons met in Bogotá and established a *Junta*, asking Bolívar to resume power and to hasten to the capital to handle the situation. Bolívar had nothing to do but to obey; it was a matter of his own conscience, even more than of the demands of the people.

He had full power in governmental matters, but he decided to exercise it with due consultation and only during the crisis through which Colombia was passing. Bogotá received him with unusual enthusiasm. He declared publicly that he would always be the champion of public liberty.

"When the people want to deprive me of the power and separate me from the command, I shall gladly submit to their will and will surrender to them my sword, my blood and my life. That is the sacred oath I utter before all the principal magistrates, and what is more, before all the people."

In truth, he used his powers with great prudence, and devoted his time especially to the reorganization of the army and the extinction of privateering, ordering that no more licenses should be issued and that those in force should be recalled.

Memorials to him were drafted in every part of Nueva Granada, and even the smallest villages showed their unanimous wish that Bolívar should take the situation in hand and save the country. Guayaquil and Venezuela did the same. It seemed that everything was settled and that peace was to last forever. Bolívar did not use the name of Dictator nor that of Supreme Chief, but the one given to him by law, *Libertador Presidente*. He regulated his own powers, created a council of state, ordered that all guarantees granted by the constitution of Cúcuta be respected, and offered to convoke the national representation for January 2, 1830, to establish at last the constitution of the Republic. In papers concerning the constitution, he expressed disgust for dictatorship.

> "Under a dictatorship, who can speak of freedom?" he said. "Let us feel mutual compassion for the people who obey and for the man who commands alone."

He was as generous as ever with his enemies. Santander was appointed minister of Colombia in Washington; and in the appointment of the members of his council of state, Bolívar did not hesitate to include men who had not shown the least friendship for him, if their intellectual achievements or their patriotic work warranted the distinction.

Santander repaid Bolívar's kindness by fostering a plot against his life. On the 25th of September, Bolívar's palace was attacked by a group of conspirators whose object was to murder him. They took the guard by surprise, wounding and killing several of its members, and started towards Bolívar's room. The Liberator intended to fight, but was persuaded that it would be foolhardy; so he jumped through the window to the street and hid for a while. The conspirators, crying, "Death to the tyrant and long life to General Santander and the constitution of Cúcuta," went in pursuit of him. Colonel William Ferguson, the Liberator's Irish aide-de-camp, seeking his chief in order to defend him, was killed. Other men were also murdered. The garrison was made ready and went to the palace. Finding it abandoned by the conspirators, it assembled in the principal square of the city and prepared to defend Bogotá. There was fighting in several sections, accompanied by much sorrow, for it was believed that Bolívar had been killed. Bolívar had not been killed, but he would have preferred death to the torture which he experienced at this reward of his eighteen years of service in the interest of his country. Seeing some soldiers pass discussing the defeat of the mutineers, Bolívar joined them and soon presented himself to the garrison, who received him with tears of joy.

To make a show of energy, he published a decree declaring that he would assume the powers given to him by the people and would use them according to circumstances; but this event had depressed him more than anything in his life. "I have really been murdered," he said. "The daggers have entered here in my heart. Is this the reward for my services to Colombia and to the independence of America? How have I offended freedom and those men? Santander has caused all this; but I will be generous."

Several of the conspirators were sentenced to die, among them Santander, but Bolívar changed the penalty to banishment from the country. Santander always contended that the sentence of death had been unjust. The worst punishment that might have fallen upon the would-be-murderers was the unanimous condemnation of all the people.

CHAPTER XIX

1829-1830: DIFFICULTIES WITH PERÚ. SLANDER AND HONORS. ON THE ROAD TO CALVARY.

The wound received by Bolívar's heart had no possible cure. His physical condition was getting worse and worse from day to day, but he had to remain in power. Serious dangers threatened the country. In Bolivia, Sucre, a victim of the conspiracy of Perúvians, had been wounded and forced to leave the country where he had been in command, but not without showing his generosity in a message to the Bolivian Congress, in which he said:

> "Although through foreign instigations I carry broken the arm w in Ayacucho put an end to the war of American Independence, which destroyed the chains of Perú and gave birth to Bolivia, I am comforted, feeling in these difficult circumstances that my conscience is of any guilt.... My Government has been distinguished by clemency, tolerance and kindness."

All of this was the naked truth. Perú had invaded Bolivia and had attacked Colombia. Bolívar immediately organized an expedition, under the command of General José Maria Córdova,—who distinguished himself in Ayacucho,—and he, himself, prepared to go immediately. After attending to several matters of an administrative character, he started towards the South, in spite of declining health. It was torture for him to ride on horseback. He knew that little of life remained for him, and still he was going to give his last days to the service of his country. He did not seek revenge on his enemies then in power in Perú. He only wanted to defend the integrity of Colombia against the foreign invader.

As was his custom, he tried first to settle all difficulties through negotiation. His aide-de-camp, Colonel O'Leary, was sent to offer the Liberator's friendship to Perú, but the Peruvian Government did not deign even to answer O'Leary's communication. In January, 1829, the Perúvians obtained some success; they occupied Guayaquil and other places with an army of over 8,000 men well organized, while the Colombians numbered only 6,000 men, poorly equipped, but commanded by the greatest of all South American generals after Bolívar,—Sucre, who was able to inflict two defeats on the enemy during the month of February, and, after his final victory, offered a capitulation, which was accepted by the enemy, with the stipulation that the boundaries between Perú and Colombia were to be settled by a special commission, and that neither of the contracting parties would intervene in the domestic affairs of the other. The city of Guayaquil was to be surrendered to Colombia. The Peruvian army was commanded by La Mar, head of the anti-Colombian party of Perú.

The inhabitants of Pasto had again rebelled against Colombia, but they were subdued without bloodshed. Upon receiving their submission, Bolívar went to Quito, where, after long separation, he met Sucre, and found in the loyal friendship of the Great Marshal of Ayacucho some comfort in the midst of all the bitterness which filled his soul. On that occasion, for the first time, Bolívar's facility and felicity of language failed him, and his tears were the only expression of his feelings. He received in Quito a manifesto issued by Páez regarding the murderous attempt of the 25th of September, once more protesting that he was loyal to Bolívar. Again mentioning the sword that his illustrious chief had given him, he said: "In my hands it will always be Bolívar's sword, not my own; let his will direct it and my arm will carry it."

La Mar, on trivial pretexts, did not surrender the city of Guayaquil, but undertook the reorganization and enlargement of his army. Bolívar prepared himself for new struggles, while in private he did his best to have the capitulation fulfilled. Advancing to Guayaquil, he succeeded in recovering without a single shot the land lost by Colombia, for La Mar had become unpopular in Perú on account of this war and was deprived of his command and expelled from the country. Immediately after his banishment public feeling in Perú expressed itself freely in favor of Colombia and a friendly arrangement was very easy. La Mar died soon after in exile, forgotten by all.

In Guayaquil, Bolívar's life was in great danger because of very serious illness, and his soul was sick of the unjust attacks by his enemies. In 1815 the Duke of Manchester, governor of Jamaica, had said of him that *the flame had consumed the oil*, but at this time it was really true. Yet on August 31st, while barely convalescing, he plunged again into activity by issuing a famous circular asking the people to express their opinions freely on the form of government and on the constitution to be adopted by the next constitutional congress. After recovering from that illness he went to Quito, where he worked in the reorganization of the southern departments, and at the end of October he left for Bogotá.

Then another man added his bit to the work of Bolívar's enemies. Córdova, tempted by ambition, and believing in the necessity for the separation of New Granada from Venezuela, claimed that, since Bolívar was getting old and had very few days to live, he should be deprived of the command. He tried to form a combination with Páez, Mariño and others. Bolívar knew of his actions and talked to him in an attempt to win back his friendship. He thought that so distinguished a general would hesitate much before smirching his glory with ingratitude; but at the bottom of his heart this wound, added to the others he had received, pushed him a little farther towards his premature end. Córdova finally raised the flag of insurrection, based on the Constitution of Cúcuta, calling Bolívar the tyrant of the country. He and his improvised army were destroyed by O'Leary, and he was fatally wounded on the field of battle. He was young, rich and endowed with great powers of attraction; he was brave and clever, and his disloyalty and insurrection form one of the saddest episodes of this part of the history of America.

It may have been of some comfort to Bolívar that at that time a special envoy from France went to Bogotá to express the esteem of his country for the great man of the South. Addressing the Council of Ministers, the French envoy, Bresson, voiced the hope of seeing Bolívar soon, and of

> "expressing to him verbally to what extent Simón Bolívar's name is honored among us. France admires in him not only that intrepidity and celerity in enterprise, that vision and that constancy which are the qualifications of a great general, but pays homage to his virtue to his political talent, which are guaranty of independence and order—the essentials of the freedom of the country, which has placed her destiny in his hands."

Europe was unanimous in her admiration for Bolívar. In England they also had the highest opinion of the American hero.

> "It is impossible," wrote the Secretary of Foreign Affairs, Dudley, in March, 1828, to Campbell, British Chargé d'Affaires in Colombia, "to have observed the events which have occurred in Colombia and its neighboring provinces since their separation from the mother country, without being convinced that the merits and services of General Bolívar entitle him to the gratitude of his fellow-citizens, and to the esteem of foreign nations."

But this general feeling also gave foundation to slanderous affirmations that Bolívar wanted to make himself king. We have seen how untrue this was. Bolívar had no other ambition than the freedom and the union of his country,—Colombia, the child of his genius. For himself, he wanted only to keep his honor untarnished and to pass his last days as a simple citizen.

During his stay in the South, the Council of Ministers started to work for a monarchy. A letter was sent to him, not speaking openly of the monarchical question, but dwelling on the restless condition of the population and the need of preparing for the future. In answer, Bolívar expressed his agreement and, knowing that he could not live much longer, said that in order to avoid civil war with its terrible results, which he expected to occur within ten years, it would be advisable to divide the country by legal and peaceable means. He declared that he considered the stability of the government impossible because of the hostility between Venezuela and Nueva Granada. He pronounced himself against a foreign monarch and said that, as for himself, he took it for granted that it was understood that he was tired of serving and of suffering ingratitude and attempts against his own life. He still insisted that, "in case no other solution seems feasible, the best way out of the difficulty would be a president for life, and a hereditary senate," as he had proposed in Guayana. In a letter to O'Leary, he wrote:

> "I cannot conceive of even the possibility of establishing a kingdom in a country which is constitutionally democratic because the lowest and most numerous classes of the people want it to be so, with an indisputable right, since legal equality is indispensable where there is physical inequality, in order to correct to a certain extent the injustice of nature. Besides, who can be a king in Colombia? Nobody, for no foreign prince would accept a throne surrounded by danger and misery, and the generals would consider it humiliating to subordinate themselves to a comrade, and resign the supreme authority forever."

He wrote that the idea of monarchy was chimerical, and that it should be discussed no more. In another letter he expressed his decision to relinquish power, whether Congress met or not.

Bolívar arrived in Bogotá on the 15th of January, 1830, and on the 20th Congress began its work under the presidency of Sucre. With the inauguration of the Congress, Bolívar considered that his public duties had ended, and in that sense he published an eloquent proclamation, which closed with this supreme appeal:

> "Fellow citizens, listen to my last words, at the end of my political career. In the name of Colombia, I beg you, I pray you, always to remain united so that you may not become the murderers of your country and your own murderers."

In this proclamation he mentioned the fact that a crown had been offered to him more than once, and that he had rejected the offers with the indignation befitting a strong Repúblican. In his message to the Congress, he offered to obey any person elected to occupy his place and to support him with his sword and all his strength.

> "The Republic will be happy," he said, "if, on accepting my resignation, you appoint as President a citizen loved by the country. She would succumb if you insisted that I command her.... Beginning today I am nothing but a citizen, armed for the defense of my country and for the

> obedience to her government. My public functions have ended forever. I deliver unto you the supreme authority which the will of the country conferred upon me."

The circular issued by Bolívar from Guayaquil on the 31st of August had been received by Páez, who circulated it in Venezuela, and organized demonstrations asking for the separation of Venezuela from Colombia. As the union of Colombia had been Bolívar's greatest conception, he was attacked, and in Valencia his ostracism was demanded. Páez was asked to prevent his entering Venezuelan territory. Wherever Páez exercised any influence, Bolívar's authority was denounced, and Páez was asked to assume the highest authority of the country. Bolívar was insulted by the press of his own nation, which called him a tyrant and a hypocrite, and insisted on his banishment. At last Páez declared himself openly. He went to Caracas, approved the rebellion of the capital against Bolívar, broke with him, declared Venezuela a sovereign state, appointed a cabinet and convoked a congress to meet in Valencia. He asked the people for subsidies for the war against Bolívar, and at the same time wrote a letter to the Libertador warning him not to oppose the will of the Venezuelans, who were ready, he said, to deliver themselves to the Spaniards rather than to Bolívar.

The Congress of Colombia had asked Bolívar to remain in command, to suppress anarchy, and to fulfil his promise that he would exercise power until the constitution had been proclaimed and magistrates duly elected. Bolívar accepted provisionally, and immediately tried to obtain a friendly compromise with Venezuela. He wanted to have a personal interview with Páez, but Páez declined. He had unsheathed the sword Bolívar had given him, and the one he had sworn to carry according to the will of the Libertador. The Congress of Colombia appointed a constitutional committee, and Bolívar proposed that a peace mission be sent to Venezuela to make known the intentions of the national representation, and to show the basis of the constitution, in order to destroy any suspicions which might have been conceived in Venezuela regarding this document. The mission was appointed, one of its members being the illustrious General Sucre, President of the Congress, another, its Vice-President. The Commissioners were asked to inform the Venezuelan people that the future constitution was to be entirely Repúblican, that the Congress hoped to obtain a friendly agreement with Venezuela, and that the Congress was firmly decided to preserve the principles of integrity of the Republic and unity of the government in the new constitution; that all dissensions were to be forgotten and that all existing differences would be settled in a friendly way. Sucre said very frankly that, considering the state of affairs in Venezuela, he did not expect favorable results. The basis of the constitution as finally adopted provided that

> "the republic should be unitary according to its fundamental law; the government should be popular, representative and elected for terms of eight years; the legislative power should be divided among the Senate, the House of Representatives and the Executive; there was to be a Council of State to help the President of the Republic, and this Council should have no responsibility except in the case of treachery; the Cabinet officers were to be responsible. Local legislatures to be created to take care of local interests; individual rights were guaranteed."[21]

Bolívar showed his generosity again by pardoning those who were in exile on account of the conspiracy of the 25th of September, and then asked permission of the Congress to be relieved of his duties because of ill health. Once obtaining permission, he went to a country place to recover. He was never again to exercise the executive authority of Colombia. Using his power, he appointed General Domingo Caicedo to take his place. He was a very kindly and patriotic man and the best suited to mediate between the contending parties.

The peace commission was not even received in Venezuelan territory, but had to stay on the border to meet the delegates appointed by Páez, one of whom was Mariño. Claiming that Bolívar was oppressing Nueva Granada, Páez had prepared himself for a campaign, not only to support the Venezuelan Revolution but to deliver Nueva Granada from its so-called oppressor. The real cause was simply his inordinate ambition. The conferences between the two groups were fruitless, and the delegates of the Congress withdrew. Meanwhile, Páez was issuing proclamation after proclamation against Bolívar, who had to leave the country place where he was caring for his health and go to Bogotá to meet the new situation. He was asked to resume the supreme command, but he knew that he was not strong enough for the task. He consulted the Ministers and some friends, but nothing was decided. Some members of the Congress wanted to elect him constitutional President; these, however, were vehemently attacked by others. Many friends deserted the Libertador, knowing perfectly well they had little to expect from a life which was rapidly nearing the end. Bolívar saw all this, learned of the intrigues of his enemies, and, convinced that the best thing he could do was to withdraw not only from power but from the country he had loved so dearly and for which he had done so much, he sent a message on the 27th of

21 Larrazábal—Vida de Bolívar. Vol. II (6th Edition), New York, 1883, p. 531.

April, 1830, to the Congress, in which he reiterated his decision not to accept again the supreme power of the state.

> "You must be assured," he said, "that the good of the country imposes on me the sacrifice of leaving forever the land which gave me life in order that my presence in Colombia may not be an obstacle to the happiness of my fellow citizens."

Three days later, Congress answered, praising the patriotic disinterestedness of Bolívar and protesting that the country would always respect and venerate him, and take care that the luster of his name should pass to posterity in a manner befitting the founder of Colombian independence.[22]

22 Upon the disruption of Colombia, Nueva Granada kept her old name. Later she changed it to Colombia. It is necessary to bear in mind that Colombia of today is only a part of Bolívar's Colombia.

CHAPTER XX

1830: FRIENDS AND FOES. SUCRE'S ASSASSINATION. THE LEES OF BITTERNESS. AN UPRIGHT MAN'S DEATH.

Bolívar prepared to go to Cartagena, where he intended to sail for Jamaica or Europe. His melancholy was relieved by a message from Quito, in which the most prominent citizens asked him to select as his residence that city, where he was respected and admired. "Come," they said, "to live in our hearts and to receive the homage of gratitude and respect due to the genius of America, the Liberator of a world." The Bishop of Quito, Monsignor Rafael Lasso, also sent a communication, in his own name and in the name of the clergy, endorsing the petition. Bolívar did not accept this invitation. On May third, the constitution of Colombia was signed, and on the following day don Joaquín Mosquera and General Domingo Caicedo were elected President and Vice-President of Colombia, respectively. Bolívar showed his pleasure at the result, and uttered the following words:

> "I am reduced to the private life which I have so much desired if the Congress wants any special proof of my blind obedience to the constitution and the laws, I am ready to give whatever may be asked."

He left the palace and went to live in a private residence. There he received a delegation of the principal citizens of Bogotá, who placed in his hands a beautiful document containing the following words, especially worthy of notice:

> "You conquered the plane upon which our future happiness will be built and, believing yourself to be an obstacle to that happiness, you resign voluntarily the first authority, protesting never again to take the reins of government. Such a noble, generous and magnanimous action places you above heroes. History has its pages filled with the actions of brave soldiers and fortunate warriors, but it can make them beautiful only with the actions of a Washington or a Bolívar. In private life, you will receive unmistakable proofs of our devotion to your person. We shall always remember your merits and services, and we shall teach our

children to pronounce your name with tender emotions of admiration and gratitude."

This document was signed on May 5, 1830, by Caicedo, the Vice-President, in the exercise of the executive power, the Archbishop of Bogotá, the members of the Cabinet and 2,000 distinguished citizens. Three days later, Bolívar left Bogotá, accompanied for six miles by the members of the Cabinet, the ministers of the diplomatic corps, many military men and citizens, and almost all the members of the foreign colonies. The following day, Congress passed a decree which is an honor to it and to Bolívar, by which homage of gratitude and admiration was paid him in the name of Colombia, and it was ordered that wherever Bolívar might choose to live he should be treated always with the respect and consideration due the first and best citizen of Colombia. In that same decree, it was ordered that a pension of 30,000 pesos per year, decreed to Bolívar in 1823, be punctually paid for life.

Among the many sad things which can be told of this man of sorrows, is the fact that this pension was sorely needed. In March of that year he had been forced to sell his silver, and even then did not have enough money to pay for his trip.

On his way to the Caribbean, Bolívar received homage in all the towns he entered. He advised everybody to respect the law and to obey the government. Every day saw him poorer. His personal fortune in Venezuela had been greatly diminished, and possessions left to him by his ancestors were involved in litigation. Consequently, he could count on very little. He had planned to sail from Cartagena, but was unable to do so. From there he endeavored to secure some money from his relatives in Caracas, in which effort he failed.

While in Cartagena he received news of several insurrections in favor of the integrity of Colombia and of himself as head of the nation. Bolívar refused to heed these calls, and continued his life of poverty, embittered and saddened by the news received that Antonio José de Sucre, his beloved friend and lieutenant, the hero of Pichincha and Ayacucho, had been murdered on his way to Quito, on the 4th of June, while crossing a mountain called Berruecos. It is difficult to conceive how Sucre could have had enemies, he who was perhaps the purest and kindest figure of all the American War of Independence, all generosity, forgiveness and benevolence. He was riding alone when shot from an ambush. His orderly, who was at some distance behind him, rushed to the scene only to find that Sucre was dead. His corpse remained there that afternoon and all night. On the following day the soldier buried him in the forest.[23]

23 Sucre's body was lost for a long while. In the Pantheon of Caracas there are three beautiful monuments: the one in the center contains Bolívar's ashes;

That news was perhaps the last blow to Bolívar. The day he received it he was attacked with a severe cold, which he neglected and which developed into his fatal illness, an illness which had been long latent in his frail body. He remarked that the murder had perturbed his spirit. As a matter of fact, from the day he received the news, he sank rapidly in both mind and body.

Venezuela was doing her best to thrust the dagger still deeper in Bolívar's heart. Since she had decided to withdraw from the Union, it was resolved by Congress that no negotiations should be exchanged between Venezuela and Nueva Granada while "General Simón Bolívar remains in the territory of old Colombia." One representative proposed, as a provision for the continued relations between Venezuela and Nueva Granada, the expulsion of General Bolívar from all the territory of Colombia, and his motion was accepted. Most of the former friends of the dying man were now his bitter enemies, all due to the ambition of Páez and the intrigues of his partisans and of those who, in good faith, believed that idealistic Repúblican principles could meet the practical needs of Colombia.

The President of Colombia, Mosquera, committed so many errors in government that he lost his prestige and was forced to leave Bogotá. The government then passed into the hands of Caicedo. A military insurrection overthrew the President and the Vice-President, and the military element proclaimed Bolívar chief of the republic, granting him full powers. General Urdaneta, old friend and constant companion of Bolívar, was entrusted provisionally with the executive power, and he organized a cabinet. He at once sent a commission to meet the Libertador in Cartagena. Many friends wrote Bolívar beseeching him to return to Bogotá to establish public order. The foreign representatives also used their influence to induce Bolívar to accept authority, for he was the only guaranty of peace.[24]

---

the one to the right, which we have already described, is devoted to Miranda; the one to the left is devoted to Sucre, and contains an expression of hope that some day Venezuela can pay homage to her great son. The body of Sucre has been found at last in Quito, and it is expected that very soon it will occupy its place near Bolívar, Sucre's leader and friend. (See: Manuel Segundo Sánchez, Los Restos de Sucre, Caracas, 1918.)

24 Among the foreign representatives who showed pleasure at the idea of Bolívar's accepting the power was the representative of the United States.

It is worthy of notice that the reputation of Bolívar as an ambitious man was discredited in the State Department at Washington by the very person thought to be its originator. When Watts was in Bogotá, in his correspondence with Clay (No. 19, Nov. 28, 1826), he asserted that he did not believe in the anti-Repúblicanism of Bolívar, who had consolidated the departments and acted with prudence and discretion. Watts expressed his firm conviction that Bolívar would not act as dictator but in conformity with the constitution, stating also the fact that Bolívar had refused the Bolivian and Peruvian dictatorships. In

Bolívar, declining to accept command of the insurrection and condemning the movement, sent General O'Leary to the assembly provisionally organized to advise them to use the right of petition and to inform them that he condemned all other actions. He reiterated his offer to serve as a citizen and as a soldier, and repeated that he would not accept any position except as the majority of the people willed. In a letter to Urdaneta he said that between him and the presidency there was "a bronze wall," which was the law. He advised them to wait until the election could be held, and said that he would then assume the executive power in case he were chosen in free elections held according to the law. This letter was the last public defense of his career. The last principle he sought to establish was the most sound of Repúblican principles.

> "The source of legality," he wrote, "is the free will of the people; not the agitation of a mutiny nor the votes of friends."

From Cartagena he went to a town called Soledad, and then to Barranquilla, where he remained during October and November, receiving daily news of the insults with which Venezuela was rewarding his services, and knowing very little of the good work of his friends, for he still had friends in several sections of the countries he had set free. All Nueva Granada was in favor of his assuming power as supreme chief of the republic. Ecuador proclaimed him father of his country and protector of

his communication of March 2, 1827 (No. 26), Watts denies the rumors of the monarchial ambitions of Bolívar, and says that he has nothing but the greatest magnanimity. On March 15, Watts himself asked Bolívar to assume power.

All these stories of disinterestedness seem to be contradicted in the correspondence of Harrison and Van Buren. In his note of May 27, 1829 (No. 13), Harrison speaks of monarchical plots, expressing his belief that Bolívar is behind them, founding his assertions only on the opposition of Bolívar to foreign princes. He is very free in speaking of *plans*, but he gives no precise data about them. In his note of July 28, 1829 (No. 18), Harrison states that the monarchists are determined to put Bolívar on the throne, and adds that he saw a letter of "*a man in high position* who has enjoyed the entire confidence of Bolívar, but who is now in complete opposition to all his schemes of personal aggrandizement." Bolívar, according to this letter, intended to become the monarch of Colombia, Perú and Bolivia. Then Harrison mentions the printing of a paper on the evils of free government, and states that that paper, of which he had seen a single copy, had the purpose of making propaganda in favor of Bolívar, but had been suppressed for fear that it would injure Bolívar's cause. All this sounds very much like personal hostility, and shows that the practice of some diplomatic representatives of making trouble for the countries where they are accredited instead of representing their own country in a dignified manner is not new.

After the correspondence of Harrison, we find the papers of Moore to Van Buren. In No. 10 of December 21, 1829, Moore affirms that Bolívar had no monarchical designs and encloses a letter of Bolívar to O'Leary, ridiculing monarchical government. That letter is dated August 21, 1829, and in it Bolívar suggests the election of another president. Moore accuses Harrison of insulting the Colombian government. The author is indebted to Dr. Julius Goebel, Jr., for the references to these papers.

Southern Colombia, and the government of Bolivia, learning that he was going to Europe, decided to appoint him its ambassador to the Holy See.

But Bolívar was preparing for his last voyage. He planned to go to Santa Marta, where his friends urged him to rest. His physician heartily approved, thinking that there his health might improve. When he arrived at Santa Marta, on the 1st of December, he had to be carried in a chair. Subsequent to an examination by a French and an American physician, he was sent to a country place called San Pedro Alejandrino, situated about three miles from Santa Marta, where he obtained temporary relief. On the 10th there were symptoms of congestion of the brain, but they disappeared. The same day he drafted his will and, not desiring to die without speaking again to his fellow citizens, issued his last proclamation, which read as follows:

> "Colombians, you have witnessed my efforts to establish freedom where tyranny formerly reigned. I have worked unselfishly, giving up my fortune and my tranquillity. I resigned the command when I was convinced that you did not trust my disinterestedness. My foes availed themselves of your credulity and trampled upon what is most sacred to me—my reputation as a lover of freedom. I have been a victim of my persecutors, who have led me to the border of the tomb. I forgive them.
>
> "Upon disappearing from your midst, my love prompts me to express my last wishes. I aspire to no other glory than the consolidation of Colombia; all must work for the invaluable blessing of union; the peoples, obeying the present government, in order to free themselves from anarchy; the ministers of the Sanctuary, by sending prayers to Heaven; and the soldiers, by using their swords to protect the sanctions of social order.
>
> "Colombians, my last wishes are for the happiness of our country. If my death can help to destroy the spirit of partisanship, and strengthen union, I shall tranquilly descend to my grave."

After this act he became delirious and, calling his servant, he said: "Joseph, let us go away. They are throwing us out of here. Where shall we go?"

On the 17th of December, at one o'clock in the afternoon, the great man of the South, one of the greatest men in the history of the world, died. On that same day, eleven years before, in Angostura, Colombia had been created by his genius. He died at the age of forty-seven and one-half years.

> "Few men have lived such a beautiful life in the whirlpool of action; nobody has died a more noble death in the peace of his bed."[25]

His death was the end of Colombia.

---

25 *Bolívar*—J.E. Rodó.

For twelve years his remains rested in Santa Marta, and then they were carried to Caracas, where they now lie in the Pantheon, between two empty coffins, that of Miranda on his right and that destined for Sucre on his left.

There the Venezuelans honor him as the protecting genius of their country. They have blotted from the memory of man the ingratitude of their forefathers. They live in constant veneration of the great man, and consider him as the creator and protector of their country, and the greatest source of inspiration to live austerely and united within Venezuela, since they cannot form a part of that greater country, the dream of which went with Bolívar to his tomb.

A patriot, a general as great as the greatest who ever lived, a statesman possessing an exceptional wisdom and a vision which has been justified by a century of American history, a loyal friend, a man of generous and liberal nature, always forgiving, always opening his arms wide to his enemies, always giving all that he had in material wealth and in spiritual gifts, a conqueror of the oppressors of his country, a founder of three nations (which later were converted into five, by the disruption of Colombia); the man who consolidated the independence of America, making his power felt as far as the provinces of the River Plata and Chile; a symbol of freedom, even in Europe where his name was like a flag to all those who fought oppression; a sincere Repúblican—all this was Simón Bolívar, and he was something more. He was the best personification of his own race, the Spanish race, which made him the brother of Morillo, Latorre and Rodil, a race which lives in twenty nations of the earth and in whose memory all names now stand equal, if they represent the same principles, whether they were written in Covadonga or Carabobo, by the sword of Pelayo or by the sword of Bolívar.

A man who writes of Bolívar's life, actions and sorrows, can hardly retain the serenity of the historian, but surrenders to that deep emotion composed of profound awe and human love, and, though his work may have been begun impersonally, it ends with the creation in his heart of those deep feelings which at times have no better expression than tears.

CHAPTER XXI

THE MAN AND HIS WORK

Bolívar was of rather less than medium height, thin and agile. In all his actions he showed quickness and alertness. He had large, black, piercing eyes, his eyebrows were curved and thick; his nose straight and long; his cheeks somewhat sunken; his mouth, not particularly well formed but expressive and graceful. From early youth his forehead was deeply lined. His neck was erect; his chest, narrow. At one period of his life he wore a mustache and sidewhiskers, but he resumed shaving about 1825, when grey hair began to appear. His hair was auburn at first, and his complexion very white in his youth, but tanned after his long campaigns. His appearance evidenced frankness of character, and his body, spiritual energy.

Bolívar was always a great reader. In his style and his quotations he shows his predilection for the classics, especially for Plutarch's "Lives." He also read much of the literature of the French Revolution. He was a very impressive orator; his addresses and proclamations show much emphasis, and the rhetorical artifice is apparent, as it is in all literature of this kind. In his letters he uses a very simple and naturally witty style. He was a great coiner of sentences, many of which can be found in his proclamations and addresses. His political perspicacity was remarkable. He could and did break the conventionalities and the political principles sacred in that epoch, to formulate those which were better for the condition of the country. He was a shrewd judge of men, and knew how to honor them and please them for the good of the cause they defended. All his intellectual power was necessary to become a master of men like Páez and Bermúdez. His mental alertness was exceptional. He could make a decision promptly without showing the effect of haste. He had a brain for large problems and for small details. He would attend to the organization of his army down to the most minute details, as well as to the preparations for long campaigns.

The most admirable moral quality of Bolívar was his constancy. It rose above everything.

His energy was marvelous to carry him through the difficulties he had to encounter. In defeat he had

> "the virtue of Antheus as no other hero had to such a degree; a singular virtue of growing to more gigantic proportions when the fall had been deepest and hardest; he had something like a strengthening power

> to assimilate the sap of adversity and of discredit, not through the lessons of experience, but through the unconscious and immediate reaction of a nature which thus fulfils its own laws. His personality as a warrior has in this characteristic the seal which individualizes it, as was aptly said in a few words by his adversary, the Spanish general Morillo: 'More fearful vanquished than victor.'"[26]

His soul could be like steel, as in the case of Piar, and it could be soft, as in his untiring forgiveness to Santander. His generosity was unlimited. He gave all. Any soldier could come to him and receive money. It is said that no common soldier went away from him with less than a dollar. When he was on his way to Cartagena, having resigned power forever, when he was writing to Caracas for money, at a time when he had not enough to pay his transportation abroad, he was still giving of his limited resources to all who begged of him.

His ambition was legitimate. In a communication he acknowledged that he was not free from all ambition; but that does not mean that he yielded to it. Virtue does not lie in the absence of temptation, but in fighting it successfully. He was truly ambitious for glory, and when glory is as legitimate as his was, there is no worthier ambition. He was accused by Lorain Petre of craving flattery, and of having been delighted with the homage paid him on his way to Potosí. Great men have been flattered always, and that they are flattered does not mean that they like flattery. Furthermore, there is a certain delicate flattery which every man likes. We, sober-minded Americans, have often heard some of our great men who are still living, even called saints, and we do not feel shocked. After having given life to three countries, one of them composed of three large divisions, Bolívar could receive homage without finding it incongruous or exaggerated.

He was refined in manner and always a gentleman. In his campaigns he was careless of his clothing through necessity, but when in the cities he liked to have all the refinements. He never thought of money; he would spend it if he had it, and if he did not spend it, he gave it away. He enjoyed society and was a great admirer of women. "He knelt before love, without surrendering his sword to it."

He was human. He enjoyed a good joke, and sometimes his jokes hurt. It is related that once, after a long march, he arrived at a small town where he expected to get some food. He was received by the notables of the town, among them a young intellectual, who took from his pocket a long address. Bolívar listened to the beginning and at once knew that it was going to be not only long but tedious. The young man came to a sentence reading: "When Caesar crossed the Rubicon...," at which point

---

26 *Bolívar*—J.E. Rodó

Bolívar interrupted him, saying, "My dear friend, when Caesar crossed the Rubicon he had had his breakfast, and I have not yet had mine. Let us first have breakfast." Generally, he respected everyone's feelings, and was much inclined to praise others, the living as well as the dead. We may well remember the honors paid to Girardot, his beautiful words in homage to Cedeño and Plaza, how Páez received his dues after the battle of Carabobo, and how Sucre was given his right place as one of the most legitimate glories of the continent by Bolívar. Speaking of Anzoátegui's death, he said: "I would have preferred the loss of two battles to the loss of Anzoátegui." No more beautiful way could be found to be generous while being just.

We have called Bolívar a gentleman; we might rather call him a knight. He loved an ideal and lived for that ideal, and that ideal was his last thought before he went to his rest.

He was judged in Europe and North America in very flattering terms. Daniel

Webster, J.H. Perkins and Joseph Story, in the name of the Bunker Hill Monument Association, wrote Bolívar the following:

> "When we read of the enormous sacrifice of personal fortune, the calmness in difficult situations, the exercise without misusing a power greater than imperial power, the repeated refusal of dictatorship, the simplicity of your Repúblican habits and the submission to the constitution and law which has so gloriously distinguished the career of Your Excellency, we believe that we see the image of our venerated Washington. At the same time that we admire and respect his virtues, we feel moved by the greatest sympathy to pay equal homage to the hero and Liberator of the South."

Martin Van Buren wrote:

> "What better example could be presented of human glory than that the great chieftain who, after having successfully resisted foreign aggression and extinguished domestic commotion, also conquered the weakness to which noble hearts have been subjected at all times."

Murray, an English rear admiral, wanted to present his homage to the "leader of all South America"; Lord Byron, whose yacht was called Bolívar, also expressed his desire to visit him. Lafayette, Monsignor de Pradt, Martin de Nancy, Martin-Maillefer, and the noted Humboldt, among others, expressed their admiration for Bolívar. Victor Hugo praised him. His name was on the lips of the Repúblicans of Europe as a symbol of liberty.

We have seen the words of Lafayette in transmitting the present sent to Bolívar by Washington's family. A former member of the French

Convention wrote to him: "You are the first citizen of the world." The noted Irish orator O'Connell sent his son to him with the following words: "I am sending him to you, illustrious sir, in order that, admiring and imitating your example he may serve under Your Excellency." The same was done by Sir Robert Wilson, member of the English Parliament. Kosciusko's nephew went to him to have the honor to serve him. The Dutch representative in Bolivia compared him with William of Nassau. Bernadotte, King of Sweden, spoke of a striking analogy between Bolívar and himself. Joseph Bonaparte, King of Spain, expressed his desire that Murat's son go to Bolívar as his aide-de-camp. Iturbide's son preferred also to serve under him. J.P. Hamilton, British commissioner to the republic of Colombia, says: "He is the greatest man, the most extraordinary character produced up to this day by the new world." He considers him "supereminent above all heroes living in the Temple of Fame."

Many persons have made comparisons between Bolívar and Napoleon, Bolívar and Washington and Bolívar and San Martín. Juan Montalvo (in "Simón Bolívar") writes that Bolívar is not so well known as Napoleon because the glamour of Napoleon's life reduced to silence the lives of his contemporaries. He asserts that in the future, Bolívar will take his place beside the French Emperor. Napoleon owes his glory to Chateaubriand, to Lamartine, to Madame de Stael, to Byron, to Victor Hugo, while Bolívar has had few biographers, and a very few have spoken of him with the power and authority of those who praised or attacked Napoleon.

Regarding a comparison between Washington and Bolívar, Montalvo says:

> "Washington presents himself to memory and imagination as a great citizen rather than as a great warrior; as a philosopher rather than as a general.... Washington and Bolívar have in common their identity of purpose; both aspired to the freedom of a country and the establishment of democracy. The difference between these two illustrious men in the excessive difficulty one had to conquer and the abundance with which the other carried on his work to the end. Bolívar, during several periods of the war, had no resources at all, nor did he know where to get them; his indestructible love for his country, the sense of honor active in his breast, the fertile imagination, the supreme will, the prodigious activities which formed his character, inspired in him wisdom to turn the impossibility into a reality.... North America was rich, civilized and powerful even before its emancipation from Mother England; if the colonists had not had their leader, one hundred Washingtons would have presented themselves to fill the place, and not at a disadvantage. Washington was surrounded

by men as remarkable as he was, if not better: Jefferson, Madison, men of great and deep counsel; Franklin, a genius of Heaven and earth. All these and many others, no matter how great they were, or how numerous, were as one in the service of the cause, were rivals in obedience.... Bolívar had to tame his lieutenants, to fight and to conquer his own fellow citizens, to fight one thousand elements conspiring against him and against independence, at the same time that he fought the Spanish legions and conquered them or was conquered by them.... Washington presents himself to the admiration of the world, more venerable and majestic, and Bolívar, higher and brighter. Washington established a republic which later became one of the greatest countries on earth; Bolívar founded also a great country, but, less happy than his elder brother, saw it crumble down; and though he did not see his work destroyed, he saw it disfigured and diminished. The successors of Washington, great citizens, philosophers and statesmen, never dreamed of tearing up the sacred mantle of their mother in order to cover their scars with rags of purple; Bolívar's companions, all of them, stabbed Colombia order to take for themselves the greatest prize. Washington, his work finished, accepted the trivial presents of his fellow citizens Bolívar refused millions offered by Perú. Washington declined a third presidential term in the United States and, like a patriarch withdrew to live tranquilly in the bosom of private life, enjoying without any mixture of hate the respect of his fellow citizens, venerated by the people and loved by his friends. This singular and happy man had no enemies. Bolívar accepted the tempting command that came to harass his spirit for the third time, and this time from an impure source, he died rejected, persecuted, insulted by many of his contemporaries. Death has erased this small blemish and we see only the light which surrounds the greatest of South Americans. Washington and Bolívar were august men, the glory of the New World."[27]

In reality, great men cannot be compared. Each one stands by himself. Washington was an able general, ready to sacrifice himself for his country; a learned man, trained in military affairs; the representative of the will of his fellow citizens, who were behind him in his tremendous fight for freedom. Washington was the Father and the servant of his country.

Bolívar did not receive special training in military affairs. He did not represent the will of his country, for his country had no will. His country really did not exist. Bolívar created it. He was obeying no commands but those of his conscience. He was making something out of nothing, and in his campaigns it was the flash of genius which led him rather than science.

Washington was successful as a military commander and more so as a statesman; Bolívar had remarkable successes and crushing defeat a general, and, as a statesman, he showed a vision which amounted to

27 "Simón Bolívar," Juan Montalvo.

inspiration—but the creation of his mind and soul, Colombia, was a sad failure. Washington lived in a country of law; Bolívar had to make the law. When Washington was absent from a place, law remained in that place; when Bolívar turned his back, law was violated.

San Martín is a noble figure. He stands alone in the southernmost part of America. He did not begrudge praise given Bolívar, whose superiority he acknowledged by withdrawing in time from the scene in America. Because of this acknowledgment, San Martín grew greater than he had been before their interview in Guayaquil. To endeavor to establish invidious comparisons between him and Bolívar does harm to both heroes and good to no one. Let both stay where they belong, in the hearts of their fellow-citizens, and in the minds of lovers of freedom.

Strong resemblance might be found between Bolívar and Lincoln. Both gave freedom to slaves; both fought a real civil war, for we must not forget that most of the royalists were Americans. Both were men of sorrows. A close examination of Bolívar's pictures and statues will reveal to the observer that in the eyes of the great man of the South is the same inexpressible melancholy which is obvious in those of our own man of sorrows, the beloved Lincoln. Bolívar was insulted and slandered as was Lincoln, and if Lincoln was assassinated by a man, Bolívar escaped the weapon of the assassin only to sink under poisonous treachery and ingratitude. It is true that Bolívar was quick-tempered, at times sharp in his repartee; his intellectual aptness had no patience with stupidity, and occasionally his remarks hurt. But when the storm had passed, he was all benevolence, enduring all, forgiving all, like Lincoln.

He compared himself with Don Quixote, and in many ways this comparison is the best. As Don Quixote, he created Dulcinea. It was not Don Quixote's fault that the lady of his thoughts, the ideal Dulcinea, proved to be just the uncouth peasant girl, Aldonza Lorenzo. Bolívar's Dulcinea was his people, and he was not to blame for all the weakness, the roughness, the grossness of those with whom he came in contact. But the American Don Quixote had a higher virtue than the knight created by Cervantes, for Don Quixote never could transform Aldonza into Dulcinea, while the peoples that Bolívar saw in his imagination, those peoples who at first were hostile to his work, through a century of constant purification, through a century during which Bolívar has become a symbol, a protecting genius, a warning against danger, an irresistible force to conquer difficulties and an imperious finger pointing to higher destinies, are approaching more and more each day what Bolívar thought they ought to be. The Aldonza Lorenzo of America, through Bolívar's sublime madness, rid of her dross, will be the Dulcinea of Bolívar's dream.

Made in the USA
Lexington, KY
18 August 2014